THE Unexplained

Survival of Death

Theories about the nature of the afterlife

Editor: Peter Brookesmith

CHARTWELL
BOOKS, INC.

ST. PHILIP'S COLLEGE LIBRARY

Acknowledgements
Photographs were supplied by Aldus Books, Associated Press, BTA, Bettman Archive, British Library, British Museum, CBS Records (Christian Steiner), Central Press, Cooper-Bridgeman Library, George E. Crouter, Culver Pictures, John Cutten, Mike Duffy/York Archaeological Trust, Robert Estall, Mary Evans Picture Library, Joel Finler, Werner Forman Archive, Leif Geiges, Thomas Gilcrease Institute, Giraudon, Jonathan Goodliffe, E.R. Gruber, Robert Harding Associates, Michael Holford Library, Robert Hunt Picture Library, Alan Hutchison Library, Mansell Collection, Musées des Beaux-Arts de Belgique, National Maritime Museum, National Portrait Gallery, Newark Museum, Peter Newark's Western Americana, Novosti, Picturepoint, Guy Lyon Playfair, Axel Poignant, Popperfoto, Psychic News, Radio Times, Rex Features, Scala, Brian Snellgrove, Society for Psychical Research, Syndication Indication, Tate Gallery, Van Duren Publishers, Frances Vargo.

Consultants:
Professor A J Ellinson
Dr J Allen Hynek
Brian Inglis
Colin Wilson

First published in the United Kingdom by
Orbis Publishing Limited 1984
Reprinted 1989 by Macdonald & Co (Publishers) Ltd

Material in this publication previously appeared in the weekly partwork *The Unexplained* © 1980–83

Macdonald & Co (Publishers) Ltd,
66-73 Shoe Lane,
London EC4P 4AB

a member of Maxwell Pergamon Publishing Corporation plc

ISBN 0-7481-0222-1

Printed and bound in Belgium

Contents

Introduction

'IT'S A FUNNY OLD WORLD,' said the great American comedian W.C. Fields, and added wryly, 'You're lucky to get out of it alive.' But of course the one thing we know for certain about life on this funny old world is that it ends in death – *our* death. And the thought of what, if anything, may greet us on the other side of that final curtain has occupied people's minds since time immemorial. Even Neanderthal man seems to have had some idea of an afterlife, and every major religion contains a belief in some kind of existence after death.

Today, perhaps more people than ever are intrigued by the question of whether we survive death in some form or other, if only because relatively few people have the comfort and certainty of religious belief to sustain them. In such a climate of doubt, it is not surprising that people have begun to look for something more like scientific evidence concerning survival – one way or other – than faith alone can provide. It is a curious fact that as religious belief began to decline in the West, so interest in psychical research began to grow. And one of the most persistent claims of psychics and mediums has been that they have been able to make contact with the souls of those who have 'passed over to the other side'. So far, the nearest we can get to a scientific approach to the question remains dependent on the evidence provided by psychics.

On the surface, it would appear perfectly logical that psychic activity should be the royal road to contact with the afterlife. For psychic activity confounds the idea that the world is limited to its physical dimensions – and suggests that even these may be far stranger than we can imagine, leaping as it does outside the normal constraints of time and space. And if we survive death, we must do so in some form that is similarly separate from our limited human bodies – for they most surely do not survive. The soul, however, is not completely divorced from the physical plane, since it is both expressed and perceived by physical means – through the medium of the body. In the same way, psychic events seem to exist on another level from physical ones, but it goes without saying that they are connected with the physical world, since we, as physical selves, can become aware of them and also because they contain *information* about the physical world (in the form of telepathy, precognition and so on) just as frequently as they purport to tell us about the life hereafter. Given these parallels between the idea of the soul and the nature of psychic events, it ought to follow that the one is an aspect of the other – or that it is something like the soul that controls or conducts psychic activity. So if the soul exists beyond the veil of death, it seems likely that we could get or stay in touch with it by psychic means.

The only question that remains is whether the evidence for survival (while undoubtedly acquired by means we understand only very imperfectly) really *is* that, or if it could be no more than a manifestation of humanity's most profound hope. This book brings together some major pieces of that evidence and tries to assess it objectively.

Certainly one of the major problems concerning the validity of the evidence is what might be termed the 'noise to signal' ratio – that is, the amount of false or misleading information that gets into communications purporting to come from the dead, as opposed to what appears to be the genuine article. But there is no reason to suppose that communication from the 'other side' is easy. The most complete statement on that subject came from the shade of Professor Frederic Myers who, frustrated at the difficulty of making himself understood, complained: 'The nearest simile I can find to express the difficulty of sending a message – is that I appear to be standing behind a sheet of frosted glass which blurs sight and deadens sound – dictating feebly to a reluctant and somewhat obtuse secretary.' This may explain another facet of communications across the great divide between living and dead: the extraordinary triviality of many of the messages. Perhaps least satisfactory – though as yet there is still no conventional explanation for them – in this respect are the 'voices' appearing on recording tape that seem to be uttered by dead people.

On the other hand, a general pattern of what happens to the soul, personality or identity after death does emerge from the mass of information that has come through to us with the help of mediums. And an extraordinary picture it is, a far cry from the traditional Christian view of birth, life, death and consequent punishment or reward in the hereafter. Instead, the nature of the hereafter is initially dependent on the *character* rather than the actions of the individual, since the 'world' he inhabits immediately after death seems to be one that he is given the opportunity to create. This can be the same in effect as heaven or hell, since the indications are that a mean-spirited person will be able to create only dreary, miserable surroundings on this 'ideo-plastic' plane (meaning created through ideas alone), while someone of a sunny and generous disposition will create a landscape appropriately happy and harmonious. The purpose of this is not merely to reward or punish, however: it is to teach.

For example, consider the case of the grossly materialistic character, whose earthly life has been spent in the pursuit of riches, Rolls-Royces and riotous living, but who has done no especial good or evil, and who has generally acted with good intentions. He will almost certainly populate his ideo-plastic plane with only the ease, luxury and sensual pleasures he sought before. While this may seem like some people's idea of paradise, its essentially self-serving nature will in time dawn on this individual, causing him to seek the spiritual dimension he so clearly lacks. Something similar will occur with the person of more obviously anti-social tendencies, so that in due course the whole purpose of existence will be made apparent. This is revealed in several stages in the afterlife, and part of the process of achieving spiritual perfection involves another spell – or perhaps many spells – in an earthly life (re-incarnation).

The ideo-plastic plane can thus be seen as something nearer a purgatory experience – though of a rather different kind from the Roman Catholic Christian notion of purgatory – than a simple, and single, judgement on an earthly life. And the other major difference from Christian teaching is that life is not itself the only chance for the soul to prove its worth. Any morality that stems from this view of existence – on either side of death – must of course be a much more complex matter than our traditional morality (which is complex enough).

It has to be objected, however, that this picture of the afterlife is remarkably optimistic, despite its complexity and subtlety. And it has to be said that there are few human beings who are prepared either to contemplate an eternity of hellfire with equanimity or to live comfortably with the proposition that life is ultimately meaningless, a kind of biological accident occurring in a cosmic and moral void. And it has to be pointed out that the fascination with the nature of the afterlife – and the concurrent desire to prove the existence of life after death – have both taken root and flourished only since the decline of organised religion in the West. In other words, if there *is* no purpose to life, we have found it necessary to *invent* a purpose, and our inventions match the times in which we live. The 'evidence' presented by paranormal means for survival of death may be, in short, no more than a rationalisation of our need to inject meaning into our lives.

This makes some of the evidence peculiarly interesting, especially that which offers to demonstrate the reality of re-incarnation. While this has been accepted doctrine in numerous Eastern religions, it has never gone down well with Christians, presumably because it can be used to escape from a sense of responsibility for one's acts. But the technique of hypnosis has produced some apparently remarkable results in probing people's minds for unconscious memories of past lives, and has probably done more than anything else in the last few decades to raise the possibility of reincarnation in the West.

More than this, the technique – known as regressive hypnosis – has also proved valuable as a form of psychotherapy. For example, a girl who had an irrational and apparently causeless fear of water was discovered under hypnosis to have had her previous life ended by drowning. Once this was pointed out to her, the fear of water disappeared. These cases are surely a strong indication of the truth of the belief in reincarnation. Unfortunately this isn't the case: the girl may have expunged her fear by finding a focus for it, however spurious, and so divorcing herself from it; once that was done, it lost its potency.

The human mind is, after all, the most creative instrument on Earth, and those of us who remember our dreams know that we *all* have the capacity to create epic stories and great dramas that our waking selves would – so to speak – never dream of. Hypnosis seems to be able to break down the barriers between our rational, conscious side and the intuitive side that surfaces in such activities as dreaming and creating works of art. And it is possible that another little-understood capacity of the individual mind – the ability to fragment into multiple personalities – may have a bearing on what occurs under regressive hypnosis. Are we, far from reliving former lives, exploring alternative but deeply suppressed personalities of our own, only dressing them up in a historical setting (perhaps to keep them from taking over in the here and now)? This would certainly explain why some of the lives described by hypnotic subjects are not simply escapist fantasies, or delusions of grandeur, but include tedious and uneventful memories as well. On the other hand, this very feature of the evidence would argue for the reality of reincarnation too. In any event, we are left with much that is bewildering and inexplicable about the human mind.

The very best evidence for the survival of the human personality after death is probably provided by the documents that have become known as the 'cross-correspondences' held by the Society for Psychical Research (SPR) in London. These involved a number of the founder members of the SPR both before and after their deaths; the peculiar feature of the communications is the tendency to pose riddles or make puns (in Classical languages as often as not) that amount to a code – one that can be broken only by reference to communications by other members of the group to different mediums. This elaborate – and deliberate – attempt to establish the reality of survival has been sadly neglected by popular writers on the subject, and receives a long-deserved summary here.

This introduction has touched only briefly on the questions that lie beyond our natural human desire to remain, in some sense, alive and sentient. What are we to make of other evidence, such as that from those remarkable people who appear to be in touch with the spirits of dead artists – and are reproducing paintings, poetry and pieces of music by some of the greatest names in those fields? How should we view the bizarre history of the Fox sisters, who founded Spiritualism? We can only invite you to read these pieces of evidence for yourself, as part of a debate that must intrigue us all until our dying day.

PETER BROOKESMITH

Death of a dream

The world was stunned when the vaunted *R101* airship crashed in flames in 1930. And the sequel was no less startling: the ship's dead captain had made contact with a famous medium. EDWARD HORTON sets the scene

Below: the *R101* lies a charred skeleton in the fields near Beauvais, France. Miraculously, its ensign still flies

Right: within two days of the disaster, medium Eileen Garrett was 'speaking' to the *R101*'s dead captain

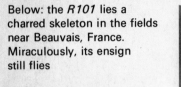

EUGENE RABOUILLE, a 57-year-old poacher, was distracted from his task of setting rabbit snares by the sound of engines overhead. He looked up into the rain-soaked night and saw a confused image of bright lights and an enormous shape illuminated by those lights. It was very low in the sky, moving slowly and falling steadily – and it was heading his way. On it came, the drone of the engines getting louder as it approached, and as Rabouille stood rooted to the spot the gigantic object suddenly pitched forward, corrected itself, and then slid almost gently into the side of a small hill about 100 yards (90 metres) from where he stood. The next moment he found himself stretched out on the ground, stunned by shock waves, deafened by noise, blinded by light.

A wall of flames shot hundreds of feet into the air, and as Rabouille picked himself up he could hear through the fire's roar terrible screams, and see in the middle of the inferno human figures rushing about, alive yet for a moment or two, but irretrievably lost. Rabouille put his hands to his eyes to shield them from the heat, and from the searing vision. Then he turned and fled. It was just after 2 a.m. on 5 October 1930.

What Rabouille had witnessed were the final moments of the British airship *R101*, and of the 48 passengers and crew who perished that rainy night near the town of Beauvais, in northern France. He had also seen the event that would crush instantly and irrevocably British faith in the whole idea of rigid airships, would spark off bitter and

lasting recriminations – and would provide the backdrop to one of the most curious episodes in the annals of psychic phenomena.

For within two days of the *R101*'s sickening destruction, no less a medium than Mrs Eileen Garrett was apparently in touch with the skipper of the enormous craft, Flight-Lieutenant H. Carmichael Irwin. Not only that, but it turned out that another airman had foretold the end of the *R101* – also from beyond the grave. And three weeks after the calamity Mrs Garrett was in contact again, this time in front of different witnesses, with the airship's dead captain.

Public fascination with these revelations was intense – naturally, as no one knew what had happened during the last few hours on board. The evidence produced by Mrs Garrett was therefore crucial not only for those who may have wanted to add ammunition to their case for survival after death, but to a question of immediate practical import. To gauge how the psychic evidence adds to both debates it is first necessary to review, in detail, the sad tale of the *R101*'s development.

In 1924 the British government had decided that the interests of a worldwide empire could be well served by the construction of a fleet of large passenger airships. Now the traditional way of going about such an enterprise would have been simply to place an order for a prototype with some suitable private firm. However, this was Britain's first Labour government, and there was strong pressure from within its ranks to give a practical demonstration of the merits of state enterprise. In the best spirit of British compromise (or fudging) the decision was reached that two airships should be built simultaneously, one by the Air Ministry

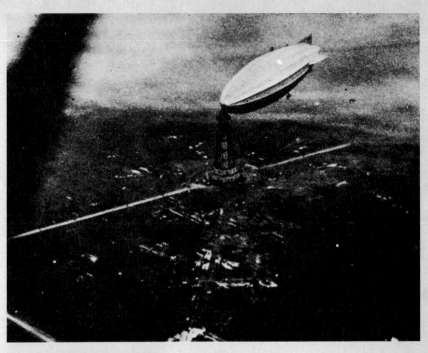

Top: the *R100* at rest after her successful flight to Montreal in July 1930

Above: Barnes Wallis, whose genius contributed so much to the success of the *R100*

Left: the *R101*, the largest airship built at that time, basks in floodlights at her mooring at Cardington. The hangar that housed her there was the biggest building in the British Empire

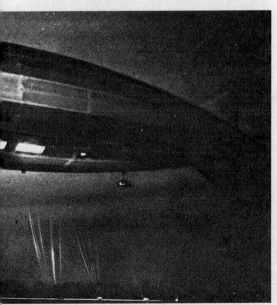

itself and the other by a Vickers subsidiary, the Airship Guarantee Company.

The specifications and standards of performance laid down for the two airships were more or less identical, and they were impressive – far in advance of any existing airship, more sophisticated even than the future *Graf Zeppelin*. They would be by a huge margin the largest airships the world had seen – kept aloft by 5 million cubic feet (140,000 cubic metres) of hydrogen. This would give them a gross lift of 150 tonnes, and with a stipulated maximum weight of 90 tonnes for the airships themselves (unloaded) they would provide a 'useful' lift of 60 tonnes – again far in advance of anything to date.

What this amounted to was a specification for a pair of airships that could transport 100 fare-paying passengers in considerable luxury to the four corners of the globe, and do so at the respectable cruising speed of 63 miles per hour (100 km/h). Altogether a grand vision, and it was by no means as fanciful as it may look in retrospect.

The Vickers team set up shop in a disused hangar at Howden, Yorkshire, and over the next five years put together an airship of the highest quality, the *R100*. They accomplished their formidable task in relative peace and quiet, away from the glare of publicity and political meddling. Meanwhile, the Air Ministry team resurrected the wartime airship base at Cardington, near Bedford. And there, unlike their rivals, they found themselves as goldfish in a bowl. How great a factor this was in the final débâcle is a matter for speculation, but what finally emerged in a blaze of public anticipation was a majestic flying coffin – the much-vaunted *R101*.

The first in the sorry catalogue of mistakes made at Cardington was probably the worst. Because of the competitive element it was

the conventional petrol type. This should have been weighed against a rather more significant disadvantage of the new diesel engines: they were far too heavy. The Howden team too experimented with diesel, saw quickly that they were too heavy and reverted to proven Rolls-Royce Condor engines. Such pragmatism was out of the question at Cardington. Considerable publicity had been given to the new diesels and they would stay, overweight or not.

The huge gasbags inside the rigid metal frame (16 of them in all) were held in place by an elaborate system of wiring. But the wiring was such that the bags continually rubbed against the girders and rivets of the framework itself. As bad, or worse even, when the airship rolled (a natural enough occurrence) the valves in the gasbags opened slightly, which meant there was an ever-present risk of highly flammable hydrogen wafting around outside the gasbags but still inside the body of the airship.

decided not to pool information with Howden. The design and construction of such advanced airships were bound to throw up problems both theoretical and practical. Original thinking would be at a premium – and there was not a lot of it in the world of British airship design in the 1920s. What the Air Ministry did – deliberately – was to dilute what little there was.

Vickers was in the enviable position of having a truly outstanding designer for the *R100* – Barnes Wallis, who was even then an acknowledged inventive genius and would later become a living legend. During the five years it took to build the two airships Wallis repeatedly suggested collaboration, but his appeals fell on deaf ears. It was almost as though the Cardington men thought they had nothing to learn from others.

Take the engines, for example. Early on it was decided in favour of a newly designed diesel type because it was marginally safer (from the standpoint of accidental fire) than

In a desperate attempt to make the *R101* effective, the enormous structure of the doomed craft is split in two to take in an extra gasbag

From bad to worse

The hurried solutions to these fundamental problems were bizarre – comical even, were it not for the dreadful outcome. There were only two ways of getting more lift: reduce the weight of the airship or increase the volume of hydrogen. The former was difficult to do to any significant degree (without scrapping the diesel engines) but the latter gave scope to fevered imaginations. Why not simply chop the airship in two and stick an extra bay in the middle? And surely there was an easy way of squeezing more hydrogen into the existing gasbags. Simply loosen the wiring to allow them to expand a little more (and chafe a little more as well). And so on. If the gasbags showed an annoying tendency to puncture themselves on bits of the framework, track down the offending projections and stick a pad over them (some 4000 pads were fitted).

The immediate results (like the final result) of this kind of folly were roughly what

Captain Hinchliffe's prediction

Even while the *R101* was stumbling toward completion, there were psychic portents of catastrophe. On 13 March 1928 a dashing war hero, Captain W. R. Hinchliffe, accompanied by heiress Elsie Mackay, took off from Cranwell aerodrome in eastern England in an attempt to fly the Atlantic. They were never seen again.

Then on 31 March, one Mrs Beatrice Earl was startled by a message that came through on her ouija board: HINCHLIFFE TELL MY WIFE I WANT TO SPEAK TO HER.

Through Conan Doyle, Mrs Earl passed the message to the aviator's

widow, Emilie, who in turn agreed to let Eileen Garrett (whom Mrs Earl knew) try to contact her dead husband. (He, incidentally, had once called Spiritualism 'total nonsense'.)

In the sessions that followed Hinchliffe's spirit became deeply concerned about the *R101*: 'I want to say something about the new airship. . . . the vessel will not stand the strain.' He pleaded that his old friend Squadron-Leader Johnston, the *R101*'s navigator, be told. But the men at Cardington were unmoved.

His last message was received as the *R101* headed for France: STORMS RISING. NOTHING BUT A MIRACLE CAN SAVE THEM. But by then, Eileen Garrett had begun to have visions of an airship in flames . . .

one might have expected. The 'new' *R101* was hauled out of the hangar to her mooring mast under perfectly tolerable weather conditions. At once, a gaping hole 140 feet (33 metres) long appeared along the top, where the fabric had merely given way. It was taped up. So was another, smaller tear that appeared the next day.

In defence of the beleaguered men at Cardington it should be said that they were working under intolerable pressure. In July 1930 the unheralded *R100*, having completed her trials successfully, flew to Montreal and back again a fortnight later. It was rumoured that only the more successful of the two airships would serve as a prototype for future development. To the rattled men at Cardington it was now vital that the *R101* demonstrate her superiority quickly. The destination for the maiden flight was India, a longer and more glamorous voyage than the *R100*'s to Montreal, and guaranteed to put Cardington back in the limelight.

Calendar of woe

So we come to the final grim chapter, and to the man who must bear most of the blame for the fiasco that cost his and many other lives: the Air Minister himself, Lord Thomson of Cardington. His devotion to the *R101* project bordered on the fanatical (his choice of title when elevated to the peerage provides a pointer). He combined this passion with unslakable ambition. His sights were set on becoming the next Viceroy of India, and by happy coincidence there was an Imperial Conference in London starting in late October. How better to draw attention to his claim than by descending on the conference fresh from a round trip to the Subcontinent aboard his beloved *R101*?

A September departure was impossible (Thomson accepted this but with ill-disguised resentment). Early October was the latest departure date that would get him to India and back in time to fulfil any of his commitments at the conference. The airship

Above: Lord Thomson of Cardington, whose driving ambition to get the *R101* into the air served only to hasten its end – and his own death

Below: the press immediately latched on to the strange aftermath of the disaster

Bottom: spectators are dwarfed by the burnt-out wreckage of the 777-foot (237-metre) long airship

must be ready by the fourth of the month because 'I have made my plans accordingly.'

Aside from the fact that the airship was unfit for such a voyage (or for a Sunday excursion) there was another hitch. It was essential to have a Certificate of Airworthiness, which could only be issued after the successful completion of exhaustive trials. But a temporary certificate was wangled, with the droll proviso that final speed trials be completed during the journey itself.

At 6.36 p.m. on 4 October the awesomely beautiful silver craft (for she was that) struggled away from her mooring mast. And it was a real struggle. Four tonnes of water (half the ballast) had to be jettisoned in those first moments, just to get airborne. Pitching and rolling, the airship that was in Lord Thomson's immortal words 'as safe as a house, except for the millionth chance' crossed low over the lights of London an hour and a half later, with one of the five engines already out of commission. At 8.21 Cardington received the laconic message: 'Over London. All well. Moderate rain.'

The last message

At 9.35 she reached the Channel at Hastings, still flying low and experiencing worse weather – hard rain and a strong south-westerly wind. Two hours later she crossed the French coast near Dieppe. At midnight Cardington received its final wireless message. After reporting the *R101*'s position as 15 miles (24 kilometres) south of Abbeville the message ended on a cosy note: 'After an excellent supper our distinguished passengers smoked a final cigar, and having sighted the French coast have now gone to bed to rest after the excitement of their leave-taking. All essential services are functioning satisfactorily. The crew have settled down to a watch-keeping routine.'

What seemed to pass unnoticed aboard the airship was her low altitude. It did not go unnoticed by some observers on the ground, one of whom was alarmed to see the gigantic craft flying overhead at an estimated 300 feet (90 metres), less than half her own length. That was about 1 a.m., and he judged her to be moving in the direction of Beauvais.

Morning Post
R101: REMARKABLE SEANCE
ONE PENNY

R101: the dead captain speaks

What exactly had brought the *R101* to its fiery end? The official inquiry could only guess – but it ignored some extraordinary evidence. For the ship's dead captain had 'come through' at an astonishing seance . . .

REPORTS OF THE CALAMITY that had befallen the *R101* began trickling into London and Cardington during the small hours of Sunday morning, 5 October 1930. At first they were guarded: even as late as 5.30 a.m. Reuters in Paris would go no further than say that 'alarm' had been caused by an 'unconfirmed report that the airship has blown up'. But this was quickly followed by the death knell: *R101* HAS EXPLODED IN FLAMES ONLY SIX SAVED.

The parallel with the sinking of the *Titanic* was inescapable – a vessel of heroic proportions, the largest and most advanced thing of its kind, safe 'but for the millionth chance' and yet hideously fated on her very first voyage. Public grief was unrestrained on both sides of the Channel.

But even in the midst of that grief some starkly insistent questions cried out for answers: how had it happened? Whose fault? A special Court of Inquiry was set for 28 October, amid angry rumours that its unspoken function would be to whitewash the Air Ministry in general and the dead Lord Thomson in particular.

As far as getting at the truth about the flight itself, and particularly what happened during those final minutes, there was a peculiar difficulty. Fate had been awkward in its selection of survivors. All the passengers were dead; so were all the officers. The only survivors were six lucky crewmen, none of whom was in the main control car (which was crushed) and none of whom was in a position therefore to know precisely how it was that the mighty *R101* kept her rendezvous with that small hillside outside Beauvais. Put

Above: the *R101* cruises over the outskirts of London during her first test flight on 15 October 1929. Thousands of sightseers had crowded Cardington to see her take to the air

Right: the captain of the *R101*, Flight-Lieutenant H. Carmichael Irwin. Would the testimony of 'his' spirit voice have helped the Court of Inquiry that investigated the tragedy?

together, their recollections of the final moments added little of importance to what Eugene Rabouille had seen from the ground.

The Court of Inquiry, sitting under the distinguished statesman Sir John Simon, delivered its verdict in April 1931. As the immediate cause of the crash the Court settled for a sudden loss of gas in one of the forward gasbags; this, if the airship were dangerously low to begin with (as she undoubtedly was) and taken in conjunction with a sudden downdraught (which was plausible) would certainly spell disaster. It was as good a guess as any.

It may well be, however, that what the Court did *not* consider in evidence was of greater significance than what it *did*. There was considerable testimony that, had it been given credence, shed a much clearer light on the disaster, and, because of its nature, on issues of vastly greater significance. It was testimony of an extraordinary kind from an extraordinary source – the dead captain of the airship.

On the afternoon of the Tuesday following the crash, four oddly assorted characters assembled at the National Laboratory of Psychical Research in West London. Harry Price, who had set up the laboratory a few years earlier, was a singular man: wealthy, mercurial, an amateur magician, a passionate investigator of psychic phenomena. And, what was of great importance in the light of what was to follow, he was a savage foe of Spiritualist hokum, whether of the deliberately fraudulent variety (which as a magician he was perfectly equipped to expose) or of the innocent type (in which genuine paranormal experiences such as telepathy were wrongly ascribed to 'voices from beyond').

One of Price's guests that day was the celebrated medium Eileen Garrett, a woman of unimpeachable integrity, whose paranormal faculties continually astonished her as much as they did those who witnessed them. Despite the fact that in trances she frequently delivered weirdly plausible messages purporting to come from beyond the grave, she refused to classify herself as a Spiritualist. And she backed up her modest mystification about her strange powers with a disarming eagerness to expose them to the most searching examinations that could be devised by the Harry Prices of this world.

The other principal guest was an Australian journalist, Ian Coster, whom Price had persuaded to sit in on what promised to be a potentially fascinating seance. Sir Arthur Conan Doyle had died a few months earlier. He and Price had wrangled for years, Conan Doyle huffy about Price's acerbic views on Spiritualism, Price discerning a credulity verging on dottiness in the celebrated author.

Conan Doyle had vowed to prove his point in the only way possible, and Price had

Above: Harry Price, who arranged the seance at which Flight-Lieutenant Irwin's 'spirit' was first heard

Below: the bodies of those killed in the disaster lie in state in flag-draped coffins, in Westminster Hall, London. Public reaction to the crash was intense: the French provided full military honours before the bodies were brought across the Channel by two Royal Navy destroyers. An estimated half million Londoners watched the funeral procession; world leaders from Hitler to the Pope sent condolences

arranged the seance with Mrs Garrett to give him his chance. Coster, a sceptic, was there as a witness. Eileen Garrett, as always, did not know the *purpose* of the seance, nor did she know who Coster was. As far as she knew it was merely one of Price's clinically controlled investigations into her strange psychic talents.

The three of them, along with a skilled shorthand writer, settled down in the darkened room, and Mrs Garrett quickly slipped into a trance. Soon she began to speak, not in her own voice but that of her regular 'control', one Uvani. He had first manifested himself years before and claimed to be an ancient Oriental whose purpose in establishing himself as a link between Mrs Garrett and departed spirits was to prove the existence of life after death. Sometimes he would relay messages in his own voice (deep, measured cadences, formal); at other times he would stand aside, as it were, and allow the spirit to communicate directly.

The uninvited spirit

Today, after announcing his presence, Uvani gave Price a few snippets of information from a dead German friend (of whom, incidentally, he was certain Eileen Garrett was perfectly ignorant), but nothing that excited him. And no Conan Doyle. Then suddenly Eileen Garrett snapped to attention, extremely agitated, tears rolling down her cheeks. Uvani's voice took on a terrible broken urgency as it spelled out the name IRVING or IRWIN. (Flight-Lieutenant H. Carmichael Irwin had captained the *R101*.) Then Uvani's voice was replaced by another, speaking in the first person and doing so in rapid staccato bursts:

'The whole bulk of the dirigible was entirely and absolutely too much for her engine capacity. Engines too heavy. It was this that made me on five occasions have to scuttle back to safety. Useful lift too small.'

The voice kept rising and falling, hysteria barely controlled, the speed of delivery that of a machine gun. Price and Coster sat riveted as a torrent of technical jargon began to tumble from the lips of Eileen Garrett.

'Gross lift computed badly. Inform control panel. And this idea of new elevators totally mad. Elevator jammed. Oil pipe plugged. This exorbitant scheme of carbon and hydrogen is entirely and absolutely wrong.'

There was more, much more, all delivered fiercely at incredible pace: '. . . never reached cruising altitude. Same in trials. Too short trials. No one knew the ship properly. Airscrews too small. Fuel injection bad and air pump failed. Cooling system bad. Bore capacity bad . . . Five occasions I have had to scuttle back – three times before starting.

'Not satisfied with feed . . . Weather bad for long flight. Fabric all water-logged and ship's nose down. Impossible to rise. Cannot trim . . . Almost scraped the roofs at Achy. At inquiry to be held later it will be found that the superstructure of the envelope contained no resilience . . . The added middle section was entirely wrong . . . too heavy . . . too much overweighted for the capacity of the engines.'

The monologue petered out at last, and Uvani came back to ring down the curtain on this portion of the astonishing seance. (In fact Conan Doyle did 'come through', but that is another story.)

Three weeks later, on the eve of the Inquiry, there began a sequel to this mystifying occurrence that was every bit as strange. Major Oliver Villiers, a much decorated survivor of aerial scraps over the Western Front, was badly shaken by the *R101* catastrophe. He had lost many friends in the crash, in particular Sir Sefton Brancker, Director of Civil Aviation and Villiers's direct superior at the Air Ministry. Indeed he had driven Brancker to the airship on the day of departure.

Villiers was entertaining a house-guest who had an interest in Spiritualism, and late one night, when his guest and the rest of the household had gone to bed, he suddenly had an overwhelming impression that Irwin was in the room with him (the two men knew each other well). Then he heard, mentally, Irwin cry out to him: 'For God's sake let me talk to you. It's all so ghastly. I must speak to you. I must.' The lament was repeated, then: 'We're all bloody murderers. For God's sake

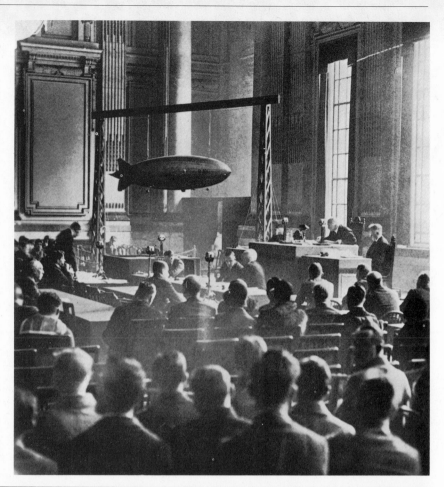

The last few minutes

None of the survivors seemed to know what had caused the *R101* to dive into the ground. One had just dozed off in his bunk when he was jolted awake by the chief coxwain rushing by shouting 'We're down lads! We're down!' Another was relaxing over a drink in the specially sealed-off smoking lounge when he felt the airship dip, dip again – and erupt into flame. Two more, in separate engine cars, were no better informed.

Engine man Joe Binks, however, had glanced out of a window only two minutes before the end, and was terrified to see the spire of Beauvais cathedral, 'almost close enough to touch'. He shouted to engineer Bell, the sixth survivor, when the floor seemed to drop away, then the ship lurched. At the same moment a message was coming through from the main control car: SLOW. Then a few moments' silence. And then the holocaust.

The Air Ministry clamped down on any news of the crash, yet in the first seance two days later 'Irwin' described how he had failed to achieve cruising height: 'Fabric all waterlogged and ship's nose down . . .'

Three survivors stand near the wreck

Left: a session of the Court of Inquiry into the disaster. Though it could not ascertain the precise cause of the crash, it had no doubts that the *R101* should never have been allowed to attempt the flight to India

Right: taken shortly before the *R101* left Cardington on its last doomed flight, this photograph shows (left to right): the navigator, Squadron-Leader E. L. Johnston, whose friend Captain Hinchliffe's spirit had allegedly warned of the inadequacies of the ship through two different mediums; Sir Sefton Brancker, who was said to have agreed to join the flight only because Lord Thomson had accused him of cowardice; Lord Thomson himself; and Lieutenant-Colonel V. C. Richmond, designer of the *R101*. All died in the final holocaust

help me to speak with you.' In the morning Villiers recounted this most disturbing experience to his guest, who promptly arranged a session with Eileen Garrett.

The first of several seances was held on 31 October and it, like its successors, took a significantly different form from the Price-Coster episode. Rather than merely listen to Irwin, Villiers conversed freely with him through Mrs Garrett. Moreover, while in the first seance Irwin came through alone, in later seances he was joined by several of his colleagues and even by Sir Sefton Brancker.

Villiers was not served by shorthand, but he claimed the gift of total recall, which in conjunction with notes hastily scribbled during the 'conversations' convinced him that the transcripts he made were virtually dead accurate. They make absorbing reading, and a short extract from the first one will give their flavour:

Villiers: Now try to tell me all that happened on Saturday and Sunday.
Irwin: She was too heavy by several tons. Too amateurish in construction. Envelope and girders not of sufficiently sound material.
Villiers: Wait a minute, old boy. Let's start at the beginning.
Irwin: Well, during the afternoon before starting, I noticed that the gas indicator was going up and down, which showed there was a leakage or escape which I could not stop or rectify any time around the valves.

Villiers: Try to explain a bit more. I don't quite understand.
Irwin: The goldbeater skins are too porous, and not strong enough. And the constant movement of the gasbags, acting like bellows, is constantly causing internal pressure of the gas, which causes a leakage, of the valves. I told the chief engineer of this. I then knew we were almost doomed. Then later on, the meteorological charts came in, and Scottie and Johnnie (fellow officers) and I had a consultation. Owing to the trouble of the gas, we knew that our only chance was to leave on the scheduled time. The weather forcast was no good. But we decided that we might cross the Channel and tie up at Le Bourget before the bad weather came. We three were absolutely scared stiff. And Scottie said to us – look here, we are in for it – but for God's sake, let's smile like damned Cheshire cats as we go on board, and leave England with a clean pair of heels.

Price and Villiers did not know one another, nor were they aware of each other's seances with Eileen Garrett. They arrived independently at the conclusion that the 'evidence' they had should be placed before Sir John Simon (Price also informed the Air Ministry). Neither the Court of Inquiry nor the Ministry was prepared to accept that these unusual happenings contributed to an understanding of the *R101* tragedy.

What was it that caused medium Eileen Garrett to pour out a flood of information about the crashed *R101*? Did the airship's dead captain really 'come through'? And just how accurate were the technical details that he gave?

THE R101 AFFAIR is a classic of its kind for two reasons. First, the messages purporting to come from Captain Irwin contained information about a matter of widespread general interest, and this information was couched in technical language. Everyone wanted to know what had happened to cause the catastrophe, and many were in a position to have informed opinions. Moreover, the official verdict of the Inquiry was not particularly convincing – composed as it was of a fair bit of speculation wrapped up in careful qualifications (necessarily, since there was not much hard evidence to go on). Someone really well informed about airships in general and the *R101* project in particular just might come to the conclusion that where Irwin's post-mortem account conflicts with the official verdict, 'his' has more the ring of truth. This could not by itself be conclusive, but it would be undeniably strong circumstantial evidence for spiritual survival.

Second, and as important as the contents of the messages, there is little to raise the question of spiritualism's chronic bugbear – the suspicion of deliberate fraud. There can be no field of investigation where the personal integrity of those 'on trial' looms larger, and therefore comes under closer scrutiny. Eileen Garrett went to her grave with an unblemished reputation. Further, the Price-Coster seance was held in circumstances

The credibility of Eileen Garrett (above) is central to the R101 mystery. She had been in touch with the 'spirit' of the aviator Hinchliffe, who uttered warnings about the airship; had had visions of an airship in flames; and received messages from the 'spirits' of those on board the R101 – seen here on its initial test flight in October 1929 cruising over St Paul's London

controlled by a world-famous detective of fraudulent mediumship. To arrange a hoax, even had he wanted to, Price would have needed to enlist as fellow-conspirators Mrs Garrett and Major Villiers, a distinguished and honourable man – and indeed several others who add weight to the assertion that there was no trickery involved.

With fraud out of the way, then, the question turns on whether the information purporting to come from the dead Irwin is of such a nature that it could have come *only* from him. Put another way, is there any possible means by which the information that came *out of* Mrs Garrett could have got *into* Mrs Garrett other than by her being in contact, through Uvani, with Irwin's spirit? If not, the case for the survival of the spirit is made – a simple conclusion, but one with profound implications.

Everything hangs on the details of the messages, therefore, and it is to them that we now turn. The case for accepting the voice as being the true Irwin has been presented in considerable detail by John G. Fuller in his book *The airmen who would not die* (1979); it runs as follows.

None of those present knew anything at all about the complexities of airship design or the business of flying one, and therefore it is impossible that such startlingly specific statements as those made by 'Irwin' – at wild

Did the spirits really speak?

speed in what was to those present a language as foreign as it is to the lay reader today – could have been dredged from the conscious or unconscious mind of any of them. That rules out straightforward telepathy.

One of 'Irwin's' statements was not only highly technical, it referred to something that would not be known outside the inner sanctum intimately involved with the airship (the new hydrogen-carbon fuel mix). Another, the reference to Achy ('almost scraped the roofs at Achy'), is just as bewildering. Price tried to find Achy in conventional atlases and maps without success. But when he tracked down a large-scale railway map of the Beauvais area (a map as detailed as the charts Irwin would have had in the control car) he found it; a tiny hamlet on the railway line a few miles north of Beauvais. Where could such a snippet of information have come from, if not from Irwin?

Finally, Price had the transcript examined, clause by clause, by an expert from Cardington (who volunteered for the job). This Will Charlton, and apparently other old Cardington hands, professed themselves astonished at the technical grasp displayed therein, and by the likelihood of Irwin's account in its essentials. Charlton reckoned that *no one* but Irwin could have been the source of this information – information that explained clearly what had happened during the fateful voyage as against the speculative account in the official report.

As far as it goes this sounds pretty convincing. But it begins to fray at the edges somewhat when it is realised that in Charlton, Price had not found an expert at all; rather a convinced Spiritualist whose claim to airship expertise rested on the shaky ground of his having been in charge of stores nd supplies at Cardington. In a review of Fuller's book for *Alpha* magazine in 1980, Archie Jarman, credited by Fuller with knowing more about the subject than any living person, draws attention to some glaring examples of Charlton's ignorance, and they are certainly of such a nature as to discredit him as an expert. For example, during the Price-Coster sitting 'Irwin' made a reference to '*SL8*'. Price had no idea what it meant, and it remained for Charlton to come up with the answer: 'The *SL8* has been verified as the number of a German airship – SL standing for Shuttle Lanz.' To track down this morsel of information Charlton had had to comb through the entire record of German airships.

Experts and amateurs

Now far from being impressive (an expert having to go to considerable lengths to discover the meaning of a reference so obscure that it could emanate only from an even greater expert such as Irwin), it is utterly damning. The *SL* stands for *Schütte Lanz* (*Schütte*, not 'Shuttle' or 'Shutte' as Fuller variously has it), the Zeppelin people's German rival in airship development before the First World War, and one of whose airships was shot down in flames in a celebrated action during an airship raid on England in 1916 (a mere 14 years before). Yet Charlton, the expert, had no idea what *SL8* referred to. It is not good enough, and Fuller makes it worse by driving home the point with a sledge-hammer: 'Charlton and his colleagues of Cardington had been strongly impressed with the reference to *SL8*. No one on the staff of Cardington could confirm this designation and number until they had looked it up in the complete records of German airships.'

Further, when Jarman was compiling a report on the affair in the early 1960s he

Eugene Rabouille, the poacher who saw the *R101* plough into the ground near Beauvais. The official inquiry into the disaster seemed, to many, to add little to his account of the great airship's final moments. The question remains: how much light does the 'spirit evidence' shed on the reasons why the *R101* crashed when she did?

solicited the opinions of two real experts: Wing-Commander Booth, who had captained the *R100* on the Montreal flight; and Wing-Commander Cave-Brown-Cave, who had been intimately involved in the *R101*'s construction.

Booth spoke for both when he replied: 'I have read the description of the Price-Irwin seance with great care and am of the opinion that the messages received do not assist in any way in determining why the airship *R101* crashed. . . .' Cave-Brown-Cave ended with the crushing comment '. . . the observations of Mr Charlton should be totally disregarded.'

Booth's verdict on the Villiers material was even harsher: 'I am in complete disagreement with almost every paragraph . . . the conversations are completely out of character, the atmosphere at Cardington is completely wrong, and the technical and handling explanation could not possibly have been messages from anyone with airship experience.' This latter is surely true. Just to take one example: in the passage quoted previously (see page 15), 'Irwin' complains about the gas indicator going up and down. Booth's trenchant reply was: 'No such instruments were fitted.'

That technical inaccuracy is bad enough but it is mild in comparison to what the officers are said to have had in mind from the moment they set off from Cardington. They supposedly knew the airship was a dud and that they had no chance of reaching their destination. But they thought they might just creep across the Channel and tie up at Le Bourget. There were only four places on Earth with the facilities to cope with such an immense airship, and Le Bourget assuredly was not one of them.

When all was lost

Then after they crossed the Channel, according to 'Irwin' they 'knew all was lost'. So what did they do? Press on into a brutal headwind hoping to make Le Bourget (knowing all was lost), 'and try at all costs some kind of landing'. An emergency landing? Like the one they made outside Beauvais? No sane person would attempt any such thing, especially when there was an obvious alternative.

If the Captain and his close colleagues really *were* terrified about the way things were going, all they had to do was turn around and with the wind at their backs limp home to the safety of Cardington. Sane men do not accept *certain* death (and commit dozens of their fellows to the same fate) rather than admit that they have been defeated by an impossible task.

Returning to the Price-Coster sitting, Mr Jarman's view is that nothing whatever occurred during the seance that cannot be put down to Mrs Garrett's own subconscious and her telepathic powers. Take Achy, for instance, at first sight so inexplicable. Not really, according to Jarman, who knew Mrs Garrett well. Apparently she frequently motored from Calais to Paris. Achy is on that road, vividly signposted. Could not Mrs Garrett have retained the name subconsciously? Since it is more than likely that the *R101* did *not* pass directly over Achy, what else are we to believe?

And while Eileen Garrett certainly knew nothing to speak of about the technicalities of airships, the *R101* was much on her mind even *before* the crash. For she had already had visions of an airship disaster, and had discussed her fears at length with none other than Sir Sefton Brancker 10 days before the accident.

The supposedly secret nature of some of the technical information provided by 'Irwin' can also be explained. The fact is that the design and construction of the *R101* (fuel mix and all) was conducted in about as much secrecy as surrounded the building of Concorde. Anyone who cared to could have amassed immense technical detail about her during those long years of building simply by

reading the newspapers. And of course the papers were full of it during the interval between the crash and the seance (Villiers had even longer to become steeped in the events that had overwhelmed his friends). As for the savage indictments of the airship that form the burden of all the seances, the Cardington follies had been notorious all along, brought to the fore, naturally, by the disaster.

Coster was a journalist, reasons Mr Jarman, and as such would be pretty well up on all this, and if we accept that Eileen Garrett had telepathic gifts we need look no further. That is a perfectly reasonable explanation, if one there be, for what Jarman himself admits is a 'mystery'.

Perhaps the final word should be left to Harry Price. In his letter to Sir John Simon, which is, incidentally, couched in the language of a disinterested research scientist, he states that he does not believe that it was the 'spirit' of Irwin present at the seance. Then he goes on: 'I must also state that I am convinced that the psychic was not consciously cheating. It is likewise improbable that one woman in a thousand would be capable of delivering, as she did, an account of the flight of an airship. . . . Where such information comes from is a problem that has baffled the world for 2000 years.'

Above: Sir Sefton Brancker, who discussed the problems of the *R101* with Eileen Garrett just before the crash

Left: the giant airship is manoeuvred by its ground crew prior to its last flight

Below: the stark, burnt-out remains of the *R101* offered no clues to the precise cause of the disaster

What happens after death?

The one great certainty for everyone is death. Yet how many of us consider – let alone prepare for – this major trauma? DAVID CHRISTIE-MURRAY discusses reasons for believing in an afterlife

WHAT HAPPENS WHEN WE DIE? Nothing? Complete bliss – 'eternal life'? Or a vague, insubstantial something?

Materialists and atheists would answer 'nothing'. For them life is a purely biological process; when the body dies the personality dies with it, just as electricity stops being generated when a battery fails. To such people life cannot 'go somewhere else'.

These rationalists frequently point out that the age-old belief in an afterlife is merely a reflection of Man's terror of death, of personal oblivion. Throughout history he has either avoided the unthinkable or surrounded it with ritual and a childish optimism. The materialist believes this to be craven and intellectually dishonest – we ought to face 'the facts' – after all, it is true to

The plains of heaven by the English painter John Martin, 1853. Hosts of the blessed rejoice in a dramatic landscape worthy of the mid-Victorian Romantic poets. These angels, some of them winged, play the traditional harp

say that the one fact of life is death.

What of the concept of 'eternal life'? Nearly all religionists have preached that we survive bodily death – in one form or another. It is probably true to say that the more sophisticated the religion, the more certainly it envisages *some* form of 'life everlasting' for some deathless element of the individual, whether in a kind of paradise or amid the torments of hell.

If the materialist is correct, no further enquiry need be made. If the religionists are correct, then it surely behoves each individual to look to his or her salvation. But in the context of religion, belief in the afterlife must remain a matter of faith, and only the experience of our own death can prove us right or wrong.

But what if neither of these rigid concepts is correct? What if something – some life-spark, vestige of the human personality – survives and enters a new kind of existence, not as a form of reward or punishment, but merely obeying a natural law? Today many

Far left: a reconstruction of the Fox family's historic home in Hydesville, New York, where the modern Spiritualist movement was born

Left: the Fox sisters, Margaretta, Catherine and Leah, from a daguerreotype taken in 1852. The strange rappings and table turnings in their home were taken by many to be the long-awaited proof of communications from the dead

psychical researchers feel that the balance of evidence suggests that 'something' does survive, not necessarily for very long after death, nor necessarily the whole personality. According to them, parts of an individual's memory-system and personality traits sometimes seem to survive for a time, enabling his disembodied self to be recognised by the living who knew him, but later perhaps to disintegrate forever.

The objective analysis of purported evidence for human survival is a major concern of the Society for Psychical Research (SPR), founded in London in 1882. But the founding of the SPR would probably never have happened but for events of a generation earlier, which themselves might never have happened but for the emancipation of Man's thought that began in the Renaissance.

Closed minds, closed ranks
As the horizons of knowledge expanded, the materialist position strengthened and by the mid 19th century a 'thinker' was generally reckoned to be someone who had freed himself from the trammels of 'superstition'. Religionists, feeling themselves under attack, tended to close their minds to facts that undermined their position, ironically adopting much the same attitude that some scientists take today when confronted with overwhelming evidence for certain paranormal events ('We don't believe in it, therefore it isn't true').

In the light of such hard rationalism, a faith with results that could be demonstrated was sought after. So when poltergeist activity occurred at the Fox family home in the small town of Hydesville, New York in 1848, the public was tremendously excited. Here at last was 'proof' of the survival of the spirit; an antidote to the bleakness of materialism. Spiritualism was born and has become a significant movement in the western world.

Spiritualists believe that their faith demonstrates incontrovertibly the existence of a life after death. They point to seances where, it is said, spirits move heavy tables, play musical instruments and introduce apports; where dead relatives and friends speak recognisably in their own voices of events known only to themselves and one or more of the sitters, and sometimes even materialise in their own appearances before them.

But scientists refused to investigate seance-room phenomena, while Spiritualists – and fundamentalist Christians – took refuge (though not as allies) in simple faith that regarded scientific discoveries as due to Devil-inspired cleverness.

It was in this climate of extremes that the SPR was founded. The founder members were a group of British intellectuals who objected to the entrenched positions of 'believers' and 'sceptics' and who felt that the objective assessment of unusual phenomena was long overdue. The material collected by the British SPR and similar societies in other countries provides the strongest clues for the serious enquirer into the question 'What happens when we die?'

The huge body of material collected since 1882 may be categorised as follows: phantasms; communications through mediums; cross-correspondences; 'drop-in' communicators; 'welcoming' phantasms seen by the dying; experiences of patients during 'clinical death'; out-of-the-body experiences; cipher and combination lock tests; appearance pacts; evidence for reincarnation; electronic voice phenomena.

Phantasms The SPR's first great achievement was a census of hallucinations. Seventeen thousand replies to a questionnaire about the prevalence of hallucinatory experiences were collected, and of these – after all possible explanations were exhausted – about 8 per cent remained as apparently genuine experiences of phantasms. These

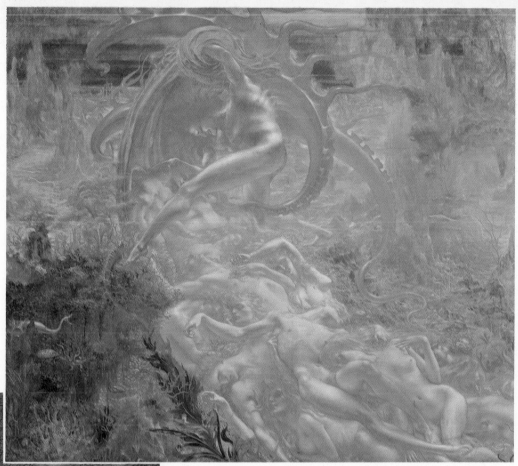

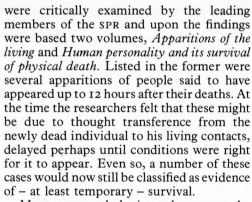

Left: *The treasures of Satan* by the late-19th-century French symbolist Jean Delville. Satan, flame-coloured as a sign of lust and of his fiery destruction of souls through degradations of the flesh, crushes his victims beneath him. Monstrous 'wings' of serpents flail about the tormented sinners

Below left: burial of the dead is not universal. Here a Red Indian brave visits the rotting corpses of members of his tribe. They have been exposed to the elements and birds of prey, on a hill set apart for the purpose. Their spirits were believed to spend eternity in the Happy Hunting Ground

were critically examined by the leading members of the SPR and upon the findings were based two volumes, *Apparitions of the living* and *Human personality and its survival of physical death*. Listed in the former were several apparitions of people said to have appeared up to 12 hours after their deaths. At the time the researchers felt that these might be due to thought transference from the newly dead individual to his living contacts, delayed perhaps until conditions were right for it to appear. Even so, a number of these cases would now still be classified as evidence of – at least temporary – survival.

Most parapsychologists who accept the evidence of phantasms at all agree that thought transference – which includes thoughts, feelings, and images both visual and auditory, and would today be classified as extra-sensory perception (ESP) – is a faculty of some human minds and could be used to explain phantasms of the living. It also seems to be confirmed by some individuals' claims that they 'think' themselves into paying 'astral visits' – travelling while out-of-the-body – to acquaintances. The claimants not only 'see' the rooms into which they project themselves mentally but report accurately such features as changes of furniture, of which their conscious selves were ignorant. Furthermore, they are often seen by the friends they 'visit' and are sometimes also accurately described by strangers.

However, some 6 or 7 per cent of the apparitions recorded in the SPR survey appeared too long after death for them to be explained as delayed telepathic communications. This small number of cases remained after all other explanations – hoaxing, exaggeration, mistaken identity, dreaming and so on – had been examined and found inadequate.

The cases that were classified as genuine apparitions or phantasms of the dead showed certain common features. In some, the apparition conveyed information previously unknown to the percipient. In others it showed a clearly defined purpose. In yet others it resembled a dead person unknown to the percipient who later recognised him from a portrait or photograph, or from some characteristic of the deceased unknown to him at the time. Sometimes different people at different times – independently of each other – saw the same apparition.

Some psychical researchers think that only those cases in which the apparitions indicate a specific purpose for their manifestation can be taken as significant evidence of survival and even then perhaps only as evidence of temporary survival. It could well be that, as a memory survives the event remembered, so a thought or anxiety to communicate something urgently to the living might continue to exist after the thinker's death until its purpose was fulfilled; then it, too, might die.

Since the early days of the SPR many astute

will communicate through the planchette board, like 'Patience Worth' (see page 48), or through automatic script (see page 52), or draw in the style of recognised masters (see page 42), or compose in the manner of famous musicians (see page 38).

Another type of sensitive is the 'direct voice' medium, who does not, as a rule, go into a trance and from whose vicinity voices of both sexes and different kinds speak in various accents, and sometimes other, identifiable languages.

Communications from these sources vary enormously in quality. Much of it is trivial and curiously materialistic. It was a frequent gibe in the early days of Spiritualism that spirits seemed to spend their afterlife smoking cigars and drinking whisky. Yet this, and other similar 'materialistic' evidence would support the teachings of some Eastern religions that an early stage after death involves passing through a realm of illusion where the ego may indulge in anything and everything it wants.

Other communications, however, are of high ethical and literary standard. Yet frequently when challenged to give an unequivocal description of what awaits us on the other side of life, communicators reply (perhaps not unreasonably) that the spirit existence is indescribable. But some rare spirits are more forthcoming, and an uncannily consistent picture of the afterlife

minds have studied and recorded evidence of survival provided by such apparitions. Some have believed that we live on, others not. It is safe to say that none of the researchers involved has been convinced of survival on the evidence of apparitions alone.

Communications through mediums. While phantasms were being investigated by the SPR so, too, were the activities of mediums – or, as they are better named, sensitives. These are people (more often women than men) who have unusual psychic talents, which they display in various ways. According to their specific gifts they are generally classified into 'mental' and 'physical' sensitives.

A 'mental' sensitive may go into a trance, in which a 'control' ('controlling spirit' or 'spirit guide') speaks through her, frequently in a voice entirely different from her own, and occasionally even giving her a different appearance, so that a European woman may temporarily take on the likeness and voice of, say, a Chinese man.

Through the sensitive the control may introduce other alleged spirits, recognisable by voice, gesture, or the nature of the private information they give to one of the sitters at the seance. Such so-called spirits may seem extremely convincing, though it must be said that those who want to believe will believe anyway. However, sensitives often have striking gifts of clairaudience, clairvoyance and other qualities of ESP. Sometimes they

Above: the 'Viking' galley is burned at the climax of the annual Up Helly A festival at Lerwick in the Shetland Isles, Scotland. The ancient Viking funerals combined cremation with dramatic spectacle, the dead being placed in a burial ship, which was set alight as it was pushed out to sea. It must have seemed to the mourners on the shore that the journey to Valhalla (the Viking heaven) was a very real one

Right: Peruvian Incas bury a chief, preparing him for an afterlife just as stylish and prosperous as his earthly life. Like many other pagan peoples, they buried food, treasure and weapons with their dead, believing the artefacts to be necessary for the dead to survive in the next world in the manner to which they were accustomed

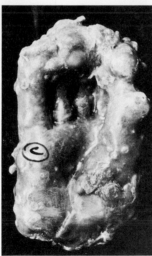

Very popular at Edwardian seances was the moulding of 'spirit' hands in paraffin wax (above); they were believed to dematerialise, leaving the moulds unbroken. But Harry Houdini, the great escape artist and scourge of fraudulent mediums, proved that it was a relatively easy trick to learn (top left)

Top right: an elaborate, pagoda-like cremation tower on the island of Bali

emerges through their communications.

'Physical' mediums are those in whose presence, whether they go into trances or not, physical phenomena occur. These may include loud raps from the seance table or from various points around the room; sometimes they seem to be in an intelligent code as if trying to convey some message. Also common are telekinetic phenomena (solid objects moving as if handled by an invisible person); levitation, of the sensitive and of objects; the playing of musical instruments by unseen hands, and actual materialisation of spirit forms.

Sadly, in the short history of Spiritualism, many of these phenomena have been faked, but there still remain many cases of genuine physical mediumship that defy 'rational' explanation. Many tests have been set up to try to trap the frauds, and, to a lesser extent, to determine the extent of the phenomena. One such was the provision of a dish of warm wax at a physical seance; the materialised 'spirit' hand dipped itself into the wax, which rapidly set. The hand dematerialised, leaving the mould unbroken.

But even such demonstrations of paranormal effects do not prove survival of death in themselves. The material accumulated by the SPR contains, so many researchers believe, far stronger evidence.

How can we possibly know if we survive death? Must it remain, as most people believe, a mystery?

'The undiscover'd

THE SOCIETY for Psychical Research (SPR) was fortunate enough in its early days to be able to call upon the services of highly intelligent, well-educated sensitives with open minds, whose names are still household words among psychical researchers: Mrs Piper, Mrs Thompson, Mrs 'Willett' (a pseudonym for Mrs Coombe-Tennant), Mrs Leonard, Mrs Garrett, among others.

Some of these were 'physical' mediums but most 'mental' – which may be significant, for physical mediums have become progressively rarer as methods of investigation have become more sophisticated. Cynics may leap to the conclusion that the likelihood of being caught as a fraud is so great these days that few dare attempt 'physical' mediumship. But an alternative view is that the very act of setting up the elaborate apparatus necessary for the investigation may inhibit the delicate, barely understood mechanism that produces the phenomena. There also seems occasionally to be an 'experimenter effect' whereby sceptical and even merely objective experimenters may have a dampening effect on the activities of the seance room.

Although the SPR's team of mediums produced some very convincing results, members of the Society were divided over the major question of proof of the afterlife. But they did agree that thought transference – including the communication of thoughts, feelings, images, sounds, even scents – had been proved beyond reasonable doubt. And although more than three decades were to pass before J. B. Rhine's work shifted the emphasis from psychical research (the scientific study of the paranormal) to parapsychology (treating psychic phenomena as expressions of little-known mental activity), extra-sensory perception, psychokinesis and general (super) ESP were already being taken as alternative explanations for the mediums' 'proof' of survival.

It is alleged that ESP explains all uncannily accurate information a medium might give a sitter, purporting to come from a dead relative. For by ESP a human mind can – almost literally – 'pick the brains' of others, without being conscious of doing so. And PK – 'mind over matter' – is the mysterious force exerted by certain gifted minds over inanimate objects. This would explain the so-called 'spirit' table turnings, rappings and so on in terms of a natural, if rare, function of the human mind. And the theory of general or super ESP is that some human minds can glean information not only from other human minds but also from any written,

Above: a soul being ferried across the river of death – the Styx – in the 16th-century painting by Joachim Patinir. It reveals a blend of Classical and Christian beliefs: the Styx and its irascible ferryman, Charon, were believed by the ancient Greeks to carry the dead to their appointed place for eternity. The dead were buried with coins in their mouths so that they could pay the ferryman. Failure to pay resulted in damnation. However the Christian conceptions of purgatory, paradise and hell are shown on either side of the dread river

ountry'

Left: Persephone and Pluto, in a detail from a Greek vase. Pluto was the ruler of Hades, or the realm of the underworld, believed by the Greeks to be a real geographical location that the dead souls reached through caves. It was a shadowy and sinister abode but not a place of active judgement or punishment. However, at a popular level there was a widespread suspicion that Hades was a much more fearsome place

printed or other kind of record (including presumably, microfilm), arrange it and produce it as a coherent account. Such a concept, if true, destroys any chance of proving survival as a fact, for any message from a deceased person – no matter how accurate or how personal the information given – could theoretically be the result of GESP. Put in Theosophical terms, this store of the sum of human knowledge is called the 'Akashic records' (Book of Life) and certain sensitive people have long been believed to have access to its 'files'. So it could be that, in some unknown way, the cross-referencing necessary for a medium to produce a convincing story of someone's life on Earth has already been done.

There are two other major arguments against evidence for survival as provided by mediums. The first is that a sensitive's so-called 'control' or 'spirit guide' may be no more than an example of the dissociated or multiple personalities that are occasionally discovered by psychiatrists. These seem to be personalities apparently formed by the splitting off of some mental processes from the mainstream of consciousness. If these 'other selves' come to the surface, they can take over completely and the condition becomes a serious illness. (There have been cases where over a dozen completely distinct personalities have inhabited the same body, either taking over in turns or fighting among themselves for possession.) And such manifestations have sometimes happened unexpectedly when apparently normal people have been hypnotised. So perhaps a sensitive, by her very nature, may be more susceptible to the development of secondary personalities than more down-to-earth, or openly sceptical, people.

The versatile forger

Add to this another extraordinary power of the human mind – *mythopoeia*. This is the extraordinary ability to create myths or detailed stories that are strikingly convincing and frequently surface during hypnotic regression as 'past lives'. It can also result in subconscious forgery, enabling some sensitives to imitate the voices, mannerisms, handwriting and even the style of musical composition or drawing of the (sometimes famous) dead. All this may be at second hand, drawn from the minds of others. Mythopoeia may also be responsible for the ability of people in trances to sing or pour out dramatically a flood of unintelligible language, known as 'speaking in tongues'. It is a theory that provides an alternative explanation for the many bizarre phenomena that have been taken as 'proof' of survival.

Cross-correspondences The deaths of the SPR's founder members, notably that of F. W. H. Myers in 1901, were followed by a new phenomenon, that of the 'cross-correspondences' from spiritualists. These were fragmentary messages received at different

group of dead SPR members. Although to a certain extent GESP could account for much of the material of the cross-correspondences, many researchers believe that they are the best evidence yet of survival. But even so, all they do is attempt to convince us, in as many ingenious ways as possible, of the continued existence of certain individuals. (The dead Myers is alleged to have found the effort of communication trying, and 'endlessly presenting my credentials' frustrating in the extreme.) But even assuming its authenticity, this massive, painstaking experiment tells us little of what happens when we die except that we retain something of our earthly habits of thought and some traits of personality.

'Drop-in' communicators Some seances have been interrupted by 'drop-in' spirits who are unknown to anyone present, yet who give information about themselves that is later discovered to be substantially correct. Again, this phenomenon can be explained by GESP, but why should a sensitive pick up information about someone in whom no one present has any interest?

'Welcoming' phantoms Witnesses of the dying often report that dead friends and relatives are apparently seen by them just before death

times and places through two or more sensitives unconnected with each other. The messages, often apparently nonsensical taken separately, made perfect sense when fitted together. The compiling of the cross-correspondences took over 30 years. The timing of their beginning, coinciding as it did with the deaths of those whose main preoccupation in life had been to understand the mysteries of death, seems to many investigators to prove beyond doubt who was behind the experiment. It seemed as if the founders of the SPR had a meeting beyond the grave and said, 'Any normal message we send will be ascribed to thought transference. Let us devise a method of communication that will not be open to such an interpretation.'

Certainly no messages easily ascribable to thought transference had ever been communicated in fragments to different mediums before. And the subject matter of the messages – poetry and erudite classical allusions – was highly characteristic of the

Above left: a soul farming in the Elysian fields. The ancient Egyptians believed the afterlife to be very similar to earthly life but more pleasurable

Above: funerary model of bakery and brewery slaves from an ancient Egyptian tomb. The model slaves were believed to assume real duties in the afterlife in the service of the master in whose tomb they were put

– coming to welcome them to the 'other side'. Perhaps these are hallucinations, a mechanism of nature to ease the passing from life. But this does not explain the cases where the dying have exclaimed at the 'visit' of a relative whose own death was unknown to them.

Clinical death Since the 1960s research has been carried out into the experiences of people who have clinically 'died' – often on the operating table – and who have come back to life. They nearly all report approximately similar experiences, whether they had previously believed in survival or not. They were conscious of leaving their

Right: an early 15th-century view of heaven as a peaceful garden. In days when life was short (and youth and beauty tragically brief), and Man very much at the mercy of the raw elements, an eternal period of relaxation in beautiful surroundings had an obvious, emotive appeal. Here the garden of heaven is shown peopled with young, healthy and attractive souls – among them a winged angel. They relax in each other's company, reading, picking choice fruits, playing musical instruments, and holding pleasant conversations. They are all dressed in the finest and most fashionable clothes. The wall suggests the exclusivity of heaven – and a sense of security after the fears of life

bodies and passing through a dark tunnel with a light at the end. When they emerged from the tunnel they were met by a radiant figure, often too bright to be seen clearly. This being they identified differently, according to their religious 'vocabulary'; for the Westerner he is usually taken to be Christ. They may also be aware of the presence of dead friends or relatives, and are filled with tremendous peace and joy. Yet they are told that their time has not yet come and they have to return. With the greatest unwillingness they re-enter their body. Significantly, people who have had this experience are never afraid of death again, seeing it as something to look forward to.

Out-of-the-body-experiences Another mass of evidence that we exist apart from our physical bodies concerns out-of-the-body-experiences which are sometimes referred to as OOBES. Many people have had the curious experience of finding themselves hovering over their sleeping – or uncon-

Above: the medieval hell was a place of brutal torment, believed to be both 'physical' and spiritual. Although sophisticated theologians of the day argued that the real anguish of hell was the knowledge that one was eternally denied the presence of God, most ordinary people believed that hell was the proverbial fiery pit. Paradoxically, it was for them a world in which the physical pain of lingering tortures was the only sort of punishment, although it was admitted that one no longer had a physical body. Sinners suffered tortures of the most sadistic nature without any hope of mercy or cessation of their pain

scious – bodies: frequently this happens in moments of crisis; during accidents, torture, or while undergoing an operation. Some people later astonish surgeons and nurses by telling them exactly what they had done and said while carrying out the operation. A few claim to be able to leave their bodies at will: and this, to them, is certain proof that they exist apart from their bodies and that this aspect of them will survive bodily death.

Ciphers and combination-lock tests A few tests have been arranged by the living so that, after their deaths, they might prove their continued existence by revealing, through mediums or friends, the solutions to puzzles. So far, none of these has been successful, though the number of the tests arranged may be too small to be significant.

Appearance pacts Lovers or friends have made pacts that the one who died first should appear to the other, perhaps under certain specific circumstances. Allegedly they have done so. But grief frequently produces hallucinations of the deceased – indeed, it seems part of the natural mourning process, acting as a comfort. Such appearances can also be categorised as crisis apparitions or similar dramatic manifestations of ESP.

Reincarnation Evidence for reincarnation not only indicates that we survive and are reborn (perhaps many times), but also offers clues as to why we are born at all. Hypnotic regression into 'past lives'; some children's spontaneous memories of being someone else; the 'far memory' of some adults; some *déjà vu* experiences; all these, though amenable to other explanations, point to reincarnation as

a possibility. Many people believe that we must submit to a string of different earthly lives until we have achieved near perfection of soul, then we become gods or progress on a purely spiritual plane of existence. Some think that not everyone is reincarnated but that we do not understand the rules governing the selection process involved.

Dr Ian Stevenson of the University of Virginia in the United States has made a detailed and scholarly investigation into the evidence for reincarnation. He has amassed hundreds of cases of alleged 'past lives' and came to the conclusion that 'a rational man . . . can believe in reincarnation on the basis of evidence.' However, for the majority of people such a belief will remain a matter of faith alone.

Electronic voice phenomena Since the 1960s tape recorders have allegedly been picking up voices of the dead. The phenomenon was discovered in this century by Jurgenson and Raudive and has since become something of a cult. However, all that can be said of it so far is that, whatever the source of the voices, they do not add to our information about the afterlife.

Despite the fast-growing interest in the paranormal and psychical research, it is true to say that the majority of believers in survival of the spirit belong to a religion, and

Above left: Buddha sits in the midst of the blessed. Stylised lotus flowers (symbols of enlightenment), peacocks, pagodas, elegant shrubs and a decorative pool are reminiscent of the Christian conception of heaven as a garden

Above right: this ancient Chinese painting depicts the Buddhist seventh hell, where the souls of the condemned are chased by ferocious dogs and devils into a deadly river

Far right: this illustration from Raphael's *The Astrologer of the 19th Century* shows a necromancer conjuring up a bloody spirit from the protection of his magic circle.

for them, a belief in the afterlife is entirely a matter of faith.

And this faith goes back a very long way; the oldest known burial customs show that ancient Man believed in survival. Even today, primitive religions take survival of bodily death for granted.

The world's more sophisticated religions, however, differ widely in their concept of Man's ultimate goal. Hindus and Buddhists teach that we escape from the miseries of earthly incarnations into a mystical and blissful unity with Brahma, the Supreme Principle, or entry into Nirvana, in which the self is lost in the infinite.

In the ancient world Greeks, Romans and Hebrews believed the spirit departed to an unsatisfactory existence in a shadowy Hades or *sheol*. Later Jews accepted the concept of the resurrection of the righteous to companionship with the patriarchs, but even today Judaism does not teach a certain doctrine of eternal life for everyone.

From ancient Egypt and Zoroastrianism the idea of judgement descended to Judaism, Christianity and Mohammedanism, with consequent doctrines of rewards and punishments, heaven, purgatory, limbo and hell.

But believer or atheist, philosopher or materialist, each one of us must die. And only then will we find out the truth for certain.

The journey of the soul

Do the souls of the dead live on? Do they go to heaven, hell, purgatory – or to some other, as yet unknown, plane of existence? And if they do continue to exist, how do we know about their experiences? PAUL BEARD surveys the evidence for the afterlife

EVEN AMONG PEOPLE who believe in some kind of an afterlife, alleged communications from the 'other side' are frequently regarded with suspicion. Perhaps it is natural to ascribe such accounts to the result of wishful thinking or unjustified hopes and fears (see page 19). For this reason most people are unaware of the enormous amount of material purporting to describe the next world from people *who are now there*. But if, for a moment, we suspend our disbelief, what emerges from this material is not only evidence for an afterlife but an amazingly consistent description of what it is like to be dead.

Obviously these accounts cannot be checked, and examining them in an open, unprejudiced way is not easy. The basic issue is one of testimony: who are the witnesses – the communicators and the living people who receive their messages?

Bearing witness

Although there are many 'communicators' and just as many 'mediums' or sensitives, not all bear the marks of good witnesses. If the dead speak to us at all, their task cannot be easy; but this does not mean that we should feel obliged to accept any communication no matter how garbled or trivial. We are entitled to listen to only the best – the most balanced, consistent and rational – accounts. In England the Society for Psychical Research (SPR) and the College for Psychic Studies have accrued a vast amount of material, which seems to emanate from intelligent and honest sources, that has been given to reputable mediums over the past 100 years or so. In the end we ourselves have to judge the communications on their own merits and on the responses they awaken in us. But a good witness is worthy of a good listener. So what do the majority of these accounts tell us?

If we do indeed survive death, then by definition the surviving part of us must already be present within us during our life on earth. The first feature of the accounts is that we do indeed take with us the same memory bank, and the same emotions and mental concepts that we had before death. We start from where we left off. But which of us survives: the tired elderly man, or the one in vigorous prime, or even the one full of illusory youthful ideals? The answer, judging by the mass of evidence, points to our having available the private, inward contents of *all* these various 'past selves'; we can reside in them temporarily, or hold on to one aspect or the other. All these imperfect selves have made us what we are; we are said to meet them all in turn again after death, in order to understand them as they really were, and profit by re-experiencing them.

A good witness is Mrs Winifred Coombe-Tennant, known in psychic circles as 'Mrs Willett'. In life she was one of the first English women JPS and a delegate to the League of Nations. She also took part as a non-professional sensitive in the cross-correspondences, which form a highlight in the multiplicity of evidence collected by the SPR (see page 58). After her death, medium Geraldine Cummins received an enormous amount of material (in the form of automatic writing) purporting to come from the discarnate Mrs Coombe-Tennant. Much of this describes the afterlife as she had experienced it. Of the 'many selves' enigma she says:

> A human being consists of a number of selves or aspects with a primary self, the total of a sum in arithmetic. . . . We only become unified in spirit on the higher level.

Dying, it seems, is not the absolute event most people fear; largely, it appears to be a state of altered consciousness. Evidence points to it being harder after death to get rid of the old earthly self than we had supposed. The same personal limitations continue until we resolve them. Death does not in itself change us; it gives us a different kind of opportunity to change ourselves.

In the seventh heaven

In spiritualistic communications, life after death is often described as a progress through seven spheres, each of a more rarified and spiritually invigorating nature than the last. The seven spheres – or mansions, or staging posts – basically represent levels of consciousness, and any of these levels is reached only by a widening and deepening of the moral nature. One is helped by teachers of superior moral stature who have progressed, so to speak, beyond the scope of recent arrivals, but who adapt themselves temporarily to make themselves understood. After death one must realise that life continues as a process of learning.

The great majority of communicators describe the death process itself as one of peacefulness and freedom from pain, even if, during the last hours, the physical body had shown every outward appearance of distress. Communicators often say this apparent pain

Left: *The garden of earthly delights* by Hieronymus Bosch. He saw the average man's ideal world as totally physical – and, ultimately, totally degrading

Below: the traditional Christian belief in a day of reckoning, as portrayed in Fra Angelico's *The day of judgement*

Bottom: T.E. Lawrence, better known as 'Lawrence of Arabia', who died in 1935. In life a brilliant yet difficult man, he was obliged to confront certain unappealing aspects of his character – 'the monk and the prig' – in the afterlife, in order to progress to higher planes

did not register with them. They say death is a gradual withdrawing, often accompanied by alternating periods of sleep or unconsciousness. Then they describe 'waking up' and being greeted by those they had deeply loved who had died previously – and also by others, familiar or not yet familiar, who will be found to know them intimately, even their secret selves. These are not angels sitting in judgement, but more highly developed spirits. Frequently an encounter with them is found to be disturbing. As one newly dead doctor of divinity is purported to have said of such a meeting:

He evidently regarded my whole life on earth – which hitherto I have thought of as being so important – as mere preparation, a preliminary to the real work I have to do here. That has been one of the greatest surprises.

Experiences are, apparently, by no means uniform, and naturally enough are partly determined by old patterns of behaviour and thinking. This first plane of experience is exactly – and literally – what you make of it. According to all communicators, the imagination is supreme; just by thinking of something it appears. Some have given this plane the term 'ideo-plastic', meaning creation through ideas alone. Some create around them past environments of home and possessions that they are unwilling to relinquish. The important key to understanding this plane is that matter is now reported to be of a finer texture, highly malleable to thought. Some, who had not believed in an afterlife, even fail to recognise they are dead. They feel they must be in a vivid dream.

But willing pupils in this environment – called the *summerland*, says the posthumous Frederic Myers – can create what they most desired on earth. But this is not 'heaven' as more enlightened communicators hasten to point out. Summerland in time shows that these 'dreams' are after all not wise enough, nor spiritual enough; they are gradually found to be too selfish and materialistic. People may find that they are seeking little more than a kind of perpetual summer holiday. Yet many accounts stress that the purpose of summerland is to enable its inhabitants to find that much of what they thought valuable is valueless.

But what sort of world does a man find around himself, if his life has been devoted to selfish gain, or if he has fallen prey to crime and violence? The habits of his mind remain the same and so, as in life, he finds he can contribute very little to his after-death environment. His self-absorption has cut him off from being able to enjoy any wider, disinterested feelings, which make up true companionship. As in the summerland his environment reflects himself – and his poverty of soul assumes an awful 'reality'. Many accounts tell of darkness, mist, bare earth and a hovel to live in. This is *winterland*.

In his continuing selfishness such a spirit often feels anger and indignation for his lot. Neither he nor others in that condition can please one another, for all are equally selfish. More unfortunately, he often treats with contempt those who enter his world from

The prophet Mohammad journeys to the seven heavens, as depicted in an early 16th-century Persian painting. The idea that the afterlife is a continuing process, involving the soul's ascent through various stages of enlightenment, is a belief common to many different religions

their own superior realms of freedom, who wish to help and teach him how to change. But frequently such a person is said to stop his ears, much as he often stopped them in life to the promptings of his conscience.

Yet it would be hard to find a man who is totally degraded, and each of these unfortunates who finds himself in winterland is there for only as long as he refuses to listen to the other, higher part of himself. Those who try to help him are really looking for this better self, however deeply overlaid. It is stressed that these individuals are not being 'punished'; their suffering stems only from their own nature as they have created it; and it is fully in their power to regenerate it. They can discover and build on their latent qualities, just as can those who find themselves in the summerland. And just as summerland is not 'heaven', neither is winterland 'hell'. Both states exist because of the individual's inner self. When he becomes more spiritual they are transcended.

Those who have outgrown the summerland state pass on to the *first heaven*. Here selfless ideals can be developed in a life shared with those who also wish to serve others. Its joys are not passive, however; they are certainly to be enjoyed, yet used strenuously to obtain growth of spiritual stature. But this level of consciousness is superior to that of the summerland. The soul is shown, step by step, its nature as it was when on earth. This self-knowledge includes the revelation and re-evaluation of all faults, errors and blindnesses – many of them, even at this stage, hard to accept. Faults easy to excuse on earth, or to hide from oneself, now show up in their true shape.

As others see us

This process is usually named the *judgement*. It is widely reported by communicators that the judgement is not made by God (as in the popular idea of 'the day of judgement'), nor by some superior being sitting in condemnation, but is in some way self-induced. To see, and then to have to condemn oneself, is painful, the more so since many faults now revealed were formerly unsuspected. The posthumous T.E. Lawrence is said to have recognised the monk and the prig in himself, which had led him to reject women's values, and brought about what he now says is a travesty of the man he could have been. The judgement shows what one has made of oneself, and it is more often than not a painful experience. But once recognised these faults can be transcended, creating a different self.

The judgement usually extends over a considerable period of experiences and adjustments; it also of course includes recognition of those qualities and actions that are worthy – in this sense life in the first heaven is part of the judgement. Though judgement is carried out by oneself, loving companions are there to explain, support and give guidance for necessary corrective steps. W. V. Blewett, a former agricultural scientist, is believed to have said, 'Here we receive absolute justice, such as can never be possible on earth.'

Motive is shown to be paramount. Hence one's actions are shown as they really were, not as one preferred to think them; and whatever joy or suffering they brought about in others is now exactly felt and experienced oneself. This can be very painful without the deadening effect of the physical body, in the same way that emotions felt in dreams – love, fear, disgust – are sharply defined as if suddenly in focus, whereas the same emotions felt in our everyday lives are muffled by the demands and stimuli of the outside world. Here there is no 'outside world' – it is all 'inside', all experienced with the awful, or beautiful, clarity of dreaming.

From what we can piece together, the various 'stages' of the afterlife can be experienced one after the other – and most frequently are – but sometimes the discarnate spirit can work at several tasks at the

Above: a Hindu statue of an *apsaras*, who is believed to gratify men's sexual desires in paradise. Most ancient religions – with the exception of puritan Christianity – imagine paradise, or heaven, to comprise endless feasting, drinking, idleness and sex in scented gardens. The indications are that the first stage of the afterlife is indeed a place where one's dreams come true

Left: William Blake's illustration for Robert Blair's *The grave*, 1813, showing the newly freed spirit rising from the shrouded corpse, keys in hand, to open the way to a blissful future

same time or go from one to the other alternately. There seems to be no rigid plan to which every person must adhere; as on earth, all people are individuals with different needs, and these are allowed for.

But most communicators express difficulty in conveying to us that their surroundings, seemingly much as on earth, are actually part of a wonderful mental world, and are much more malleable to thought than dense earth matter. All is permeated by the thoughts, feelings and beliefs of those at a common level of consciousness. The mental-emotional environment to which one belongs is not isolated, however; it is also influenced or 'played upon' by the consciousness of

those at higher levels, in a way that is as sustaining and invigorating as sunlight.

How far and how much we can see is, as always, bounded by our own limited consciousness; being played upon from higher levels is aimed at helping us gradually to enlarge our vision, somewhat in the way we learn on earth from a teacher's entire personality and not merely from the facts he passes on. But exactly what is learned on this plane is difficult for us to imagine. It can hardly be of a mechanical or practical nature for physical objects no longer exist. And it is unlikely, in the circumstances, to entail philosophical discussion about the 'nature of life'. Learning must be confined to lessons of a moral or spiritual nature, as indeed many communicators describe. But such a formidable course of study begins only when the student is ready – and eager – for it.

Each succeeding level is shut off from us until we are in a fit state to appreciate it. It is possible that some souls never rise above the 'summer holiday' plane of the summerland. It seems more likely, however, that everyone progresses to higher planes, but at his or her own pace.

These events – life in the summerland, winterland, the first heaven, and the process of the judgement – form what is meant by the 'astral' or 'desire' world of consciousness. Each man now begins to learn that it is necessary to leave this plane behind, to shed it in order to win the freedom to dwell in the most spiritual parts of himself.

Surrender of the self

The experience that many believe now awaits him is known as the *second death*. Each must now gradually become as willing to yield up his present values as, in very many cases, he was ready in the end to shed his earthly body on death. His desires in the astral world, however much they have included love of others, good fellowship and companionship, have also, as he now begins to see with certainty, really largely centred upon himself. Even when he loved others, much of this was for his own emotional satisfaction. Now in the second death he sheds all he has valued; his achievements and all the things he has won in the desire world (of which earth too is a part) have now to be given up. His gifts no longer exist for him but for the glory of God. Conan Doyle, in describing his own posthumous experience, calls this transition 'terrible and marvellous', adding that 'there are no trimmings on a man after the second death.' Yet this traumatic experience prepares the student, shorn of his most dearly held pretensions, for the next stage in his progress. Through this he can begin to find his 'true self'; a larger, more complete being – one, he discovers, for which he has always been searching.

Far from resting in peace, it is claimed that the dead lead a strenuous and purposeful existence; in fact that they are more 'alive' than we are.

IF DEATH IS NOT the end of man's personality, but rather the beginning of a sort of 'pilgrim's progress' as many psychical researchers claim, then what are the stages of this adventure? The discarnate spirit, after meeting the loved ones who had died before him, lives first in summerland or winterland (see page 31), both of which he creates from his own habits of thought, good or bad. These are both on the *ideo-plastic* plane and seem to serve to break him of his earthly preoccupations and make him yearn for the benefits of higher, more spiritual faculties. But he must first undergo the judgement and the second death, processes that hold a mirror up to the person he was, mercilessly stripping him of his illusions about himself and making him realise – by momentarily *becoming* other people in his life – what his actions and words had done to them.

Through experiencing the shattering but

Above: the Hindu deity Vishnu reincarnates for the second time – as a turtle. Belief in the transmigration of souls, or reincarnation as man or animal, is still common in the East. But, according to the alleged evidence for the afterlife, man is always reincarnated as another human being

Right: the ninth hell as described in Dante's *Inferno* and illustrated by Gustave Doré. In this wasteland of ice and desolation, the damned soul is frozen forever, unless he confesses his sins to the superior souls who visit him

ultimately rewarding process of the second death the spirit 'earns' his entry into the *second heaven*. What has been shed in the trauma is only, he discovers, his outer self, his personality, which had seemed so essential in his earth life. Personality is derived from the Latin *persona*, meaning 'actor's mask'; having cast this away during the second death he can emerge as his real, 'undivided self'.

The purpose of the second heaven is, apparently, to enable the questing spirit to grow and develop. The process takes place in what many accounts call 'the great silence'. During this period one's former identity dissolves away and one experiences a sense of great peace. One no longer knows who or where one is, but this is not in any way distressing, any more than it is 'distressing' for a butterfly to undergo the natural process of emerging from its cocoon.

Kinship of the spirit
At this point the spirit loses contact with all those he had known during his earth life. This is a temporary phase but apparently essential if he is to concentrate his energies on coping with the new, immeasurably broader landscape he now faces. There are now highly significant meetings with others, men and women with whom one feels a deep spiritual link and an intimate familiarity. This is reported as being like meeting old friends on earth with whom one has shared profound experiences. However, the spirits on this plane, although they are indeed old friends, belong to relationships formed over many lifetimes. And this one fact is central to the understanding of the whole nature of the afterlife. With those friends from long ago the spirit relives ancient memories, memories to which his immediately previous personality had no access. Together the members of the reunion relive past events they had shared, and as they do so they begin to see a distinct purpose and meaning emerge

experienced before, or perhaps at last the spirit has overcome a lengthy pattern of mistakes. Frances Banks said, 'It is still a continuation, a sequel. There is a definite continuing thread.'

This enrichment of the soul through the revelations of the past is the first step in the process of reassessment carried on in the second heaven. There are two other, equally important steps.

The first involves advice from wiser beings on how to deal with one's future earth life. The second step clarifies the true nature of the spirit's relationship with his peers, those 'old friends' with whom he has just been reunited. He now realises that they are all bound together for all eternity, united with the same overall purpose. Together they form part of a highly important unit known as a *group soul*. It is said that to be with its members is to feel a deep spiritual homecoming.

The members of an earth family may be spiritually close or they may simply be genetically linked – effectively strangers on

Most ancient cultures believed in a supernatural deity whose sole task was to preside over the dead. Part custodian and part judge, he is usually shown as a terrible figure, such as Yamantaka, Tibetan lord of the dead (above) or the Totonac god of ancient Mexico, Mictlantecuhtli (right)

from the apparently disparate and fragmentary personalities they had been in the past. Each soul has been reincarnated many times.

They now see that their lives are in no way arbitrary; they form part of a pattern and purpose that are still being worked out. Each is slowly awakening towards recognition of, and participating in, what is named his *causal self*. This carries within it the seeds of each former life but also contains hints of what is to come in future incarnations. The second heaven is both retrospective and prospective; a plane of insight into both past and future. As the posthumous Frances Banks, a former Anglican nun, is claimed to have said, it is 'the initial stage of a journey into light, during which the surviving entity is gradually reunited with the whole soul.' And now he sees his past earth life in its true perspective; not, as he perhaps thought as he was actually living it, that it was the 'be all and end all', but that it was only a tiny fragment of a much larger prospect.

The past life is only the latest chapter in a long book, the 'story' of which can stretch back over many earth centuries. As the spirit begins to witness the unfolding panorama of his lives he will inevitably realise that much in his past life was the direct consequence of actions from other, previous incarnations. Nothing is meaningless – now at last he knows the answer to the question every person asks at some point: 'Why me?'

There are many incarnations for most spirits, for almost everyone needs many chances to learn all the necessary lessons. All the opportunities will be there over the centuries for everyone. Not everyone will profit by his experience or learn at the same rate but there are many chances to put right mistakes made or opportunities lost. Perhaps the failures of the last life are similar to those

The statue of Justice that stands above the Old Bailey, Britain's foremost criminal court. The scales and the sword she carries represent the two aspects of justice: mercy and retribution. Absolute justice, however, is said to be found only in the afterlife – where motives are seen for what they really were in life. During the judgement the soul suffers the pain and humiliation he once inflicted on others. He learns for himself – the hard way – the effects of his every word and deed. But his kindnesses are also relived and rewarded

any deeper level. Their spiritual 'family' is elsewhere. Such people are said to be the true foundlings. But in the afterlife there are no such random or loose ties; the group soul comprises only members who are totally committed to their particular long-term spiritual assignment under the leadership of one who can perhaps best be called an elder brother. The individual members of each group are responsible to each other – and to the world – in order to fulfil the special task assigned them when their group was created.

Life goes on

If these narratives that claim to describe conditions in the afterlife – and, indeed, the purpose of life itself – are true, then our individual lives on earth can be seen in proper perspective, as part of a much greater plan. And although these accounts seem basically in harmony with the conventional Christian belief in purgatory, hell and heaven, the approximately similar states exist, not as final punishments or rewards for a single earth life, but as stages in a continuing education. Each has to redeem those parts of himself that are bound by the chains of his own creation. Even in the second heaven the processes of self-cleansing and selfless service continue. Here the spirit learns that there are further states of bliss, but these are too intense for it yet.

It becomes plain that life on earth and life between incarnations simply provide different opportunities of 'growing up'. Each spirit will pass from hard work to refreshment and from refreshment to further tasks – and although on the planes beyond the surroundings are said to be more pleasant than on earth, basically the work is just as strenuous. It takes enormous effort for each spirit to make any lasting progress, but he is not alone and can expect the kind of help, advice and inspiration that would have been impossible on earth. Encouraged and inspired, the individual can progress towards his own ultimate maturity.

The destiny of each soul will be fulfilled, say the communicators, only when that of the

The man who would be king

Death is said to be 'the great leveller' and nowhere is this shown more clearly than in *A Tudor story* by the late Canon W. S. Pakenham-Walsh. This purports to tell the tale of the Canon's relationship – through several mediums – with various members of the Tudor court from the early 1920s to his death at the age of 92 in 1960. Pakenham-Walsh found that his main spiritual mission was to aid Henry VIII himself, who was angry, lost and clinging pathetically to a crown he no longer possessed, and could therefore make no progress in the afterlife.

One medium had to remind 'Henry' that he was king no longer. He was furious, saying 'I am a king. I carry royal birth and death in my hands. . . . A king does not commit acts for which he is sorry.'

The Canon enlisted the help of the 'spirits' of Anne Boleyn and Elizabeth I among others, while also praying for the King's soul himself. For a time Henry vacillated between apparent repentance and humility and outbursts of regal temperament. The breakthrough came when he was allowed to meet his sons – including the baby who had been stillborn, now grown up. Henry's last communication was: 'Know that Henry, once King of England, did repent.'

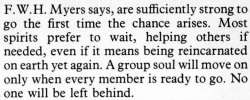

F.W.H. Myers says, are sufficiently strong to go the first time the chance arises. Most spirits prefer to wait, helping others if needed, even if it means being reincarnated on earth yet again. A group soul will move on only when every member is ready to go. No one will be left behind.

People frequently deplore the injustice of 'life', meaning their earthly existence. But if the accounts of the afterlife summarised above are substantially true, then there is such a thing as absolute justice, there is cause for hope, there is free will and ever-expanding consciousness. The narratives purporting to come from people in the after-life can be examined by anyone – religious beliefs and pious hopes aside – as evidence. Perhaps the last words of Mary, Queen of Scots, 'In my end is my beginning', express the literal truth for everyone.

group soul is completed. This may take aeons. There are many group souls, said to range from comparatively few members to many hundreds. Frequently a person's inner urge on earth is a reflection of the quest of his group soul, his equivalent of the Holy Grail. Everyone retains his free will to depart from the group soul's set path, but the promptings of his own inner nature will, it is believed, eventually lead him back to it.

During his stay in the second heaven the spirit learns from the 'replay' of his past lives to discover his true potential and what steps he should take to fulfil it. Strengthened by the insight and love of his companions he is now ready for a yet further expansion of his consciousness, which takes place in the *third heaven*. This is, however, too intense an experience for many spirits to endure for very long, although it is open to them for precisely as long as they can endure. Although almost impossible for us to under-stand, communicators tell us that in the third heaven a spirit comes to the limits of his consciousness. After a brief glimpse of this plane he finds he cannot go further into it than his nature allows. Faced with his limita-tions he has no choice but to return to earth.

Other lives, other worlds

However, if his next incarnation goes well and he grows spiritually as a result, he will find that he can then proceed deeper into the third heaven. This in turn will enable him to make more of his succeeding earth life, for it is in the third heaven that the true nature of the group soul's task unfolds as consciousness expands in the individual members.

But what happens when a person has little more to learn from earth? Most accounts agree that a choice awaits him. He can take a leap into the great unknown, leaving this planet and its successive incarnations alto-gether, and begin again somewhere else. Com-munications are vague on this point, but they do seem to imply a new cycle of physical lives on another planet. Few, the posthumous

Above: a bark painting by the Australian Aborigine artist Bunia, showing the afterlife

Right: an early 15th-century representation of St Peter receiving three souls at the gates of heaven. In the traditional Christian view, admission to heaven was in itself a kind of judgement, although the dreadful day of judgement was still to come

Below: a wall painting at Tepantitla, Mexico, dating back more than 1000 years. It is believed to show the rain god's paradise

The latest works of Beethoven, Brahms and Liszt

Many sensitives claim to receive works of art from long-dead artists – composers, authors, painters. But, asks LYNN PICKNETT, are these works truly from beyond the grave, or do they come from the subconscious mind?

BEETHOVEN IS STILL WORKING on his 10th Symphony. This extraordinary concept – that musicians and other creative beings can still produce works of art years, even centuries, after their death – is as natural as breathing to many spiritualists and psychics.

The best known of the mediums who claim to be amanuenses for long-dead composers is London housewife Rosemary Brown, who acts almost as an agent for Liszt, Beethoven, Brahms, Debussy, Chopin, Schubert and, more recently, Stravinsky. She is an unassuming, middle-aged lady with only a rudimentary musical background and she is the first to acknowledge that the works 'dictated' to her are beyond her everyday musical capacity. Mrs Brown sees herself merely as the humble scribe and friend of the late composers – the ultimate polish must come from the professionals in performance.

The idea of survival beyond death is not, however, strange to this Balham housewife. As a young girl she had visions of an elderly man who told her repeatedly that he and other great composers would befriend her and teach her their wonderful music. It

Above left: Rosemary Brown being filmed by an American television company in October 1980. During the filming Rosemary 'wrote' *Mazurka in D flat* (above), which she claims was inspired by Chopin (above right)

Left: Beethoven contacted Rosemary Brown in 1964; he told her he was no longer deaf and could once again enjoy listening to music

far beyond her conscious capacity or even her conscious knowledge. During the writing sessions Mrs Brown chats familiarly with her unseen guests, so sincerely and normally that it is difficult to be embarrassed, despite the bizarre circumstances. Pen poised over the music sheets, she listens. 'I see . . .', she says to Franz Liszt, 'these two bars go here . . . no, I see, I'm sorry. No, you're going too fast for me. If you could just repeat . . .' With pauses for checking and some conversation with the composer, she writes down the work far faster than most musicians could possibly compose.

Sometimes communications are interrupted as she gently chides Liszt for becoming so excited that he speaks volubly in German or French. Chopin occasionally forgets himself and speaks to her in his native Polish – which she writes down phonetically and has translated by a Polish friend.

So are these posthumous works recognisably those of Liszt, Chopin, Beethoven,

Below right: American composer and conductor Leonard Bernstein. Rosemary Brown sought an interview with Bernstein on the advice of her 'spirits'. He was most impressed with the music Rosemary showed him

was only many years later, when she was a widow concerned mainly with the struggle of bringing up two children on very limited means, that she saw a picture of Franz Liszt (1811–1886) and recognised him as her ghostly friend.

In 1964 she was contacted by other great composers – including Beethoven and Chopin – and her life work began in earnest: taking down their 'unfinished symphonies' and sharing her belief that there is no death – the great musicians are still producing.

The pieces transmitted to her are no mere outlines: they are full compositions, mainly for the piano but some for full orchestras. Mrs Brown says the music is already composed when it is communicated to her: the musicians simply dictate it as fast as she can write it down.

Indeed, observers of the process are amazed at the speed with which Rosemary Brown writes the music – and the standard is

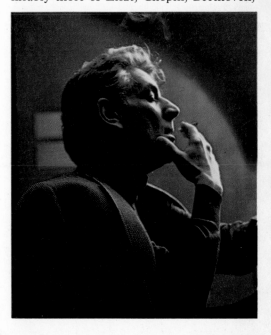

Brahms? Concert pianist Hephzibah Menuhin said 'I look at these manuscripts with immense respect. Each piece is distinctly in the composer's style.' Leonard Bernstein and his wife entertained Mrs Brown in their London hotel suite and were very impressed both by her sincerity and by the music she took to them purportedly from the long-dead composers. British composer Richard Rodney Bennett said: 'A lot of people can improvise, but you couldn't fake music like this without years of training. I couldn't have faked some of the Beethoven myself.'

Since that memorable breakthrough in 1964 Mrs Brown has also, she says, been contacted by dead artists, poets, playwrights, philosophers and scientists. Vincent van Gogh (1853–1890) has communicated his current works through her; at first in charcoal ('because that's all I had') and then in

Right: Franz Liszt, who first appeared to Rosemary Brown when she was a young girl. He told her that, when she grew up, he and other composers would contact her and teach her their music.

oils. Debussy has chosen to paint through Mrs Brown, rather than compose because his artistic interests have changed since he has 'passed over'.

Bertrand Russell, philosopher, has had to reconsider his atheism and disbelief in a life after death, for, as Rosemary Brown points out, he is very much 'alive' these days and wants to pass on the message of hope in eternal life. Albert Einstein also communicates, patiently explaining any difficult jargon or concepts, reinforcing the belief in further planes of existence.

Sceptics point out that the music alleged to come from the minds of the great composers is less than their best, being often reminiscent of their earliest, rather than their mature, works. This, says Mrs Brown, is not the point. Her first introduction to Franz Liszt was 'more than a musical breakthrough.' The late Sir Donald Tovey is believed to have explained the motivation behind the communications in this posthumous statement:

In communicating through music and conversation, an organized group of musicians, who have departed from

Rosemary Brown's contacts are not confined to the field of music: Van Gogh inspired this drawing (right) in 1975, and Debussy (below), now more interested in visual art, also paints 'through' her. She was contacted by Albert Einstein (bottom) in 1967, and by Bertrand Russell (below left) in 1973

your world, are attempting to establish a precept for humanity, i.e., that physical death is a transition from one state of consciousness to another wherein one retains one's individuality . . . We are not transmitting music to Rosemary Brown simply for the sake of offering possible pleasure in listening thereto; it is the implications relevant to this phenomenon which we hope will stimulate sensible and sensitive interest and stir many who are intelligent and impartial to consider and explore the unknown of man's mind and psyche. When man has plumbed the mysterious depths of his veiled consciousness, he will then be able to soar to correspondingly greater heights.

Mrs Brown has many friends and admirers outside the spiritualist circle, notably among distinguished musicians, writers and broadcasters. Whatever the source of her mysterious music, this modest and religious lady inspires respect and affection, so obvious is her sincerity.

She is, however, not unique in her musical communications. The British concert pianist, John Lill, also claims an other-worldly inspiration for his playing. This winner of the prestigious Tchaikovsky Piano Competition had a tough beginning, playing the piano in pubs in London's East End. As he says 'I don't go around like a crazed fellow with my head in the air . . . [I'm] neither a nutter nor some quaint loony falling around in a state of trance.' But, as he added thoughtfully, 'because something is rare it doesn't mean that it doesn't exist.'

The 'something' began for him when he was practising in the Moscow Conservatoire

Right: concert pianist John Lill is convinced that he has had spiritual help in his career. He believes that Beethoven watched him practising for the Tchaikovsky Piano Competition in Moscow, and has since held several conversations with him. And Beethoven has dedicated a piece of his own music to him – the *Sonata in E Minor* communicated to Rosemary Brown in 1972

Below: Clifford Enticknap, who has written an oratorio entitled *Beyond the veil* 'under the inspiration' of G. F. Handel (bottom)

for the Tchaikovsky Piano Competition. He became aware of a figure watching him – someone wearing unusual clothes. He believes he was being observed by Beethoven, who has since held many conversations with him. However John Lill does not consider himself a special case. This sort of direct inspiration, he says, is available to everyone who achieves a certain frame of mind:

'It is very difficult to conceive inspiration unless it is something you receive. I don't see it as something from within a person. When I go on stage I close my mind to what I have learnt and open it fully in the expectation that inspiration will be received.'

But sometimes it is difficult to achieve this state of mind 'if it's a particularly muggy day, or the acoustics are dry. Even the attitude of the audience makes a difference. A quiet mind is essential.'

Inspiration, says Lill, is an infinite thing: 'music begins where words leave off – where music leaves off the "force" begins'.

The composer of, among other magnificent works, the *Messiah* is still 'writing' grand oratorios through his medium Clifford Enticknap, an Englishman who has always been obsessed with Handel and Handelian music. Handel taught him music in another incarnation, says Enticknap, and their relationship as master and pupil dates back to the time of Atlantis where Handel was a great teacher known as Joseph Arkos. Yet before that the soul we know as Handel lived on Jupiter, the planet of music, together with all the souls we know as the great musicians (and some we may never know for they will not be incarnated on Earth).

In his personality as 'the master Handel', the musician communicated to Enticknap a

four-and-a-half-hour long oratorio entitled *Beyond the veil*; a 73-minute excerpt of this has been recorded by the London Symphony Orchestra and the Handelian Foundation Choir and is available on tape through the Handelian Foundation as 'proof' of Handel's survival beyond death.

In BBC-TV's programme *Spirits from the past*, shown on 12 August 1980, snatches from the oratorio were played over scenes of Mr Enticknap playing the organ in Handel's favourite English church. Television critics found little fault with the music – which did indeed sound to the untutored ear to be very similar to Handel's more familiar works – but the words provoked widespread ridicule. One critic compared them with the unfortunate poetry of William McGonagall (1805–1902) whose poetic sincerity was matched only by his total lack of talent and sheer genius in juxtaposing the risible with the pathetic. (Another critic went so far as to exclaim: 'Fame at last for McGonagall – he's teamed up with Handel beyond the veil!')

However, mediums warn against judging spirit communications in a state of flippant scepticism. As John Lill says of the difficulties the spirits have in 'getting through': 'It's all to do with cleaning a window, and some windows are cleaner than others.'

If, as many serious researchers into the paranormal have believed, the music does not in fact come from the minds of deceased musicians, then where does it come from? Certainly not from the conscious mind of Mrs Brown, who obviously struggles to keep up with the dictation.

Some psychics believe that our deeper inspirations are culled from the 'Akashic records' or 'Book of life', wherein lies all knowledge. In certain states of mind, and in some especially sensitive people, this hidden knowledge becomes available to the human consciousness. Mrs Brown could well be one of these specially receptive people and the music she believes comes from Chopin or Beethoven may come instead from this 'pool' of musical knowledge. Because of her personal humility her conscious mind may dramatise her method of receiving the music as direct dictation from the masters.

The late Mrs Rosalind Heywood, researcher into the paranormal and author of *The sixth sense*, has another suggestion. Mrs Brown is, she guesses, 'the type of sensitive whom frustration, often artistic, drives to the automatic production of material beyond their conscious capacity.'

To those who believe in the omniscience of the human subconscious the compositions given to the world by Mrs Brown and others like her raise more questions than they answer. But it is all so beautifully simple to the mediums – there is no death and genius is eternal.

A gallery of psychic art

Does artistic genius die with the artist – or does it survive, to find expression through the hands of living sensitives?

PABLO PICASSO, who died in April 1973, produced several drawings in both pen-and-ink and colour, three months afterwards. Perhaps it would be more accurate to say that Picasso-style drawings were transmitted through British psychic Matthew Manning, who had been trying to 'get through' to Picasso. While concentrating on him he had found his hand being controlled – apparently by the spirit of Picasso, or whatever signed itself 'Picasso' on the drawing.

Psychic art presents many of the same questions to the psychical researcher that are posed by the prize-winning literature of Patience Worth (see page 48) or Beethoven's 1980 symphony. Is the painting, poetry or music, believed by many to be

Above: the style is unmistakably Aubrey Beardsley's but this pen-and-ink drawing was produced through the hands of English psychic Matthew Manning

Above right: a posthumous Picasso. Matthew Manning remarked on the 'energy and impatience' of the artist. Picasso was one of the few artists who chose to use colour

evidence of the artists' survival beyond the grave, merely an exhibition of the medium's own repressed creativity, finally finding expression? Or is it really as simple as the psychics would have us believe – that the world's great musicians, writers and artists are 'proving' their continued existence by carrying on their arts through selected 'sensitives'?

But some examples of 'automatic' or psychic art are impressive, both in their own right and, more significantly, as examples of the styles of the great painters. Some collections of psychic art are also impressive in their diversity of style and their sheer quantity.

It was Matthew Manning's enormous collection of sketches, paintings and drawings,

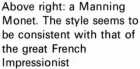

Above right: a Manning Monet. The style seems to be consistent with that of the great French Impressionist

Right: when this sketch of a hanged man began to take shape Matthew felt physically ill and wanted to stop the drawing, but his (anonymous) communicator compelled him to finish it

produced psychically by him as a teenager in the early 1970s, that convinced his publisher that he was a very special young man.

Matthew Manning's intelligent, articulate and objective approach to all the strange phenomena in his life makes fascinating reading. In his first book, *The link*, he discusses his method of 'contacting' dead artists. He simply sat quietly with a pad and pen in his hand and concentrated on the artist. He never went into a trance and was always aware of everything going on around him. Almost immediately the pen would begin to move, usually starting in the centre of the page and finally filling the page with what seemed like a well-planned work of art. Almost always the result was recognisably in the style of the artist he had been concentrating on – sometimes it was even signed. Occasionally, although bearing a strong resemblance to the style of the artist he had wanted to 'get through' to, the pictures were not signed. It seemed to Mr Manning that some other discarnate artist, perhaps even a pupil of the greater one, had intervened.

The communicators showed very distinct personalities. 'No other communicator tires me out as much as Picasso does,' said Mr Manning. 'After only a few minutes, the time it takes him to do one drawing, I feel worn out and cannot continue for at least 24 hours . . .' When Picasso first came through in 1973, Matthew Manning says his hand was 'moved with excessive force' and two of his finer pen-nibs were snapped. When the drawing suddenly stopped, completed, and Matthew looked at the picture objectively he could see that it 'was unmistakably in Picasso's style; it was bold and strong.'

Also, Pablo Picasso was one of the few

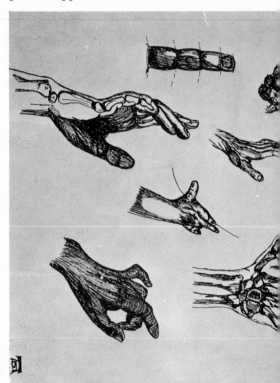

communicators who was not confused about using colour – he directed Matthew Manning's hand to pick out certain felt-tipped pens from a box of mixed colours. Most of his other discarnate artists used pen-and-ink.

Among the signed works in his collection are drawings recognisably in the styles of Arthur Rackham, Paul Klee, Leonardo da Vinci, Albrecht Dürer, Aubrey Beardsley, Beatrix Potter, Pablo Picasso, Keble Martin and the Elizabethan miniaturist Isaac Oliver.

Sometimes a finished picture would be very similar to a famous work by that particular artist. Matthew Manning often recognised them as 'copies' but occasionally the remarkable similarities had to be pointed out to him. A virtual reproduction of Beardsley's famous *Salome*, for example, took place under his eyes as he concentrated on Beardsley. But what value did these copies have – except to prove perhaps that the artist was alive and his style unchanged? Were they meant, in fact, to establish his identity?

The 'new' work came at an incredible speed. There was no preliminary sketching, nor – except in the case of Aubrey Beardsley

Above: four centuries after his death Isaac Oliver, the Elizabethan miniaturist, executed and signed such detailed – and typical – work via Matthew Manning

Albrecht Dürer (1471–1528), inventor of engraving and true son of the Renaissance, was another of Matthew Manning's alleged communicators. The rhinoceros (above right) and the study of human hands (right) – 'transmitted through' Matthew Manning – are characteristic of Dürer's minute observation and the scope of his interests

– were any mistakes made and covered over. It took between one and two hours to produce a finished work, whereas most living artists would take perhaps six or eight hours to produce a painting of similar size and complexity – and then not necessarily of the same high quality. More time would also have been spent in planning and sketching.

But one psychic artist has produced new 'old masters' at the rate of 21 in 75 minutes. In March 1978 the Brazilian Luiz Gasparetto appeared on BBC-TV's *Nationwide*

RHINOCERVS

Right: a crayon drawing by Brazilian trance artist Luiz Antonio Gasparetto in the style of Henri de Toulouse-Lautrec (1864–1901). Whereas most of Luiz's paintings take only a few minutes to complete, this one took several hours. The drawing was made in 1978 while the medium was living in London, studying English

Spiritualist medium Coral Polge presented this psychic sketch of 'a little girl' (right) to a sitter. In fact 'she' bears a striking resemblance to Dag Hammarskjöld when young (far right): the sitter was researching for a book about him at the time

Two of Luiz Gasparetto's crayon drawings in distinctly different styles: one very reminiscent of Modigliani's style (below) and a charming study (below right) that is actually signed 'Renoir'

and was seen by millions to go into a trance and produce 21 pictures – sometimes working with both hands simultaneously on two separate pictures, sometimes producing perfect paintings, but executing them upside down – and all so fast that many viewers believed the BBC had accelerated the film. And the results were apparently 'new' Renoirs, Cézannes and Picassos.

Senhor Gasparetto found working under the harsh studio lights very trying, because he normally paints – in a trance – in the dark or, at the most, in a very weak light. As he is also a psychologist by profession, he views what he produces with some objectivity. But, although familiar with others who write or

Sometimes painted with both hands simultaneously, sometimes with his toes and almost always within a few minutes, Luiz Gasparetto's trance-paintings bear striking resemblances to the works of famous, dead artists. Often the 'spirit' paintings are signed, such as this typical Van Gogh (right) – signed 'Vincent' – and this slightly unusual Picasso (far right). Others need no signature; the style is sufficient. Who else could have painted this closely-observed portrait of a *demi-mondaine* (below) but ⊃ulouse-Lautrec?

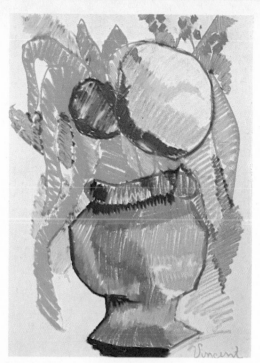

paint by psychic means, he says: 'I've never seen anyone else who can draw with both hands in the dark – in 30 different styles.' In a state of normal consciousness he says he cannot paint at all.

The Brazilian says he sees, senses and talks to all the great artists who 'come through'. Interestingly, in view of Matthew Manning's experience, Senhor Gasparetto said: 'Picasso sometimes used to be violent. If anyone whispered he would throw the paper away.'

Luiz Gasparetto travels extensively with journalist and fellow Spiritist Elsie Dubugras, giving demonstrations of psychic painting. After each session the paintings are auctioned and the proceeds go to charity.

Although Senhor Gasparetto is still producing vast numbers of psychic paintings, Matthew Manning has done little automatic art or writing since adolescence. At first he did it because he found it quelled the poltergeist activity that seemed always to surround him, but now the power, whatever it is, has been harnessed for healing.

There are some mediums, such as Frank Leah, Coral Polge and Margaret Bevan, who have produced drawings of the spirits who come to comfort the bereaved; in many cases these 'spirit portraits' of loved ones are startling likenesses.

Researchers and sceptics alike have come up with theories of repressed creativity, or even a secondary personality, to account for the strange phenomenon of psychic art. Perhaps we will never know how or why it happens, but out of all the vast array of paranormal phenomena this threatens no one – and often produces works of great beauty.

The riddle of Patience Worth

The ouija board has picked up many strange messages from the spirit world, but when 'Patience Worth' came through she produced literature of remarkably high quality.

On January 30, 1925, Patience Worth gave the following inscription for "Hope Trueblood"—

"Ye see I hae witched thee by strummin' the tenderest chord in womankind, the mither-chord. Ye see I hae witched thee by a wee lassie who lived laughin' through woein'. . . . This be the sest o' life—Pennin' wit aneath the cowl o' sorrow."

HOPE TRUEBLOOD

"A Mid-Victorian Novel by a Pre-Victorian Writer"

By PATIENCE WORTH

Edited by CASPER S. YOST

Hope Trueblood differs materially from the previous productions of Patience Worth. In this she abandons her archaic dialect and constructs her story in standard English of the present day, free from grammatical irregularities. Modern in its language, the story is relatively modern in its time, which is about the middle of the nineteenth century—"a mid-Victorian novel by a pre-Victorian writer."

It is a simple tale of life in an English village, the autobiography of Hope Trueblood, born in that village without the knowledge of a father and suffering the tortures which that stain applies to a sensitive soul in a narrow community. One gets but a glimpse of Hope's mother, but the sweetness of her personality is a dominating influence throughout the story. It is filled with a delightful mingling of humor and pathos, and it has the quality of apparent reality that is so remarkable in "The Sorry Tale." A tantalizing mystery holds the reader in suspense to the end of the tale. There are vivid sketches of scenes, and there is much characteristic beauty of thought and of diction.

Patience Worth Publishing Co., Inc.
31 Tiffany Place, Brooklyn, New York City.

TELKA

An Idyl of Medieval England

By
PATIENCE WORTH

AUTHOR OF "THE SORRY TALE," "HOPE TRUEBLOOD," "LIGHT FROM BEYOND" (SELECTED POEMS), "PATIENCE WORTH" (WITH SPIRIT PORTRAIT), "PATIENCE THE WHEEL," "THE POT UPON," ETC.

Edited with a Preface by
HERMAN BEHR

NEW YORK
PATIENCE WORTH PUBLISHING CO., INC.
1928
LONDON

TWO RESPECTABLE LADIES placed their hands lightly on the ouija board and waited – humbly hoping for some message from recently deceased relatives. It was May 1913, the town was St Louis in the southern state of Missouri, and the two ladies were a Mrs Hutchings and her friend, Mrs Pearl Curran.

The pointer of the ouija board began to move, apparently struggling to spell out a certain name. 'Pat-C, Pat-C, Pat-C . . .' it insisted, while the ladies turned the name over in their minds in bewilderment. Mrs Curran's husband John, who was also in the room, suggested that it might be a deceased Irishman. Come to think of it, Mr Curran went on (with perhaps just a hint of a twinkle in his eye), he had once known a Pat McQuillan. Immediately, the late Mr McQuillan seemed to take over the board for a time, cursing mildly to give plausibility t the character of a 'vivid Hibernian'.

However, Mr Curran, contemptuous of what he saw as the ladies' gullibility, had invented Pat McQuillan and was naturally amused to see his fictitious Irishman swear at them. But 'Pat-C', once unhindered by the pranks of Mr Curran, was to come through again – and establish herself as one of the most prolific post-mortem authors in the remarkable history of 'automatic writing'.

On 22 June 'Pat' returned and spelt out a pretty but obscure paragraph: 'Oh, why let sorrow steel thy heart? Thy bosom is but its foster-mother, the world its cradle and the loving home its grave.' Not the utterance of an imaginary Irishman this time, but it proved to be an auspicious beginning to a lengthy and, indeed, celebrated partnership between Mrs Curran and the unknown 'writer'. Pat announced herself quite clearly on 8 July, when 'the board seemed to possess unusual strength', as 'Patience Worth'.

At first Patience Worth was reluctant to give any information about herself or her past life on Earth – or, indeed, her present situation (a common enough phenomenon in the seance room). She merely contented herself with spelling out such quaint advice as: 'Thine own barley corn may weevil, but thee'lt crib thy neighbour's and sack his shelling.' Mrs Curran, fascinated by the phenomenon, was nevertheless bewildered by these rustic sayings and often spoke sharply to Patience, requesting understandable English and a clearer 'message'.

Eventually Patience Worth told how she had been born in Dorset in the 17th century. She had been raised as a good Quaker girl, humbly working in the fields and busying herself with domestic chores, until her family emigrated to America. Not long afterwards, Patience was killed by Indians.

A clearer picture was hard to come by, for

Above: American Indians attacking European settlers in the 17th century. Patience Worth claimed she had been born in Dorset in the 17th century, emigrated as a Quaker to the New World, and been killed by Indians. But if questioned further about her earthly life she was consistently reticent

Patience apparently enjoyed her life on Earth so little that she could hardly bring herself to recall it. Perhaps such a short and unfulfilling life was not worth remembering, especially as – now she had 'found' Mrs Curran – she had an opportunity to make up for lost time.

From 1913 until Mrs Curran's death in 1938 Patience Worth 'dictated' a colossal number of words, mostly of a quality that can fairly be described as 'literary'. Some of this output was in the quaint English that she had first used, some was in a more modern, readable style. Her speed was enormous: one evening she produced 22 poems. In five years she 'wrote' 1,600,000 words through the mediumship of Mrs Curran.

Psychic bestseller

If sheer volume of words were the most remarkable aspect of this case, we might never have heard about it. Yet more staggering were the variety and quality of what Patience Worth wrote. She composed poems, novels and plays. One of her full-length novels, *Hope Trueblood*, was published in England under the name 'Patience Worth', with no explanation of the bizarre circumstances surrounding its composition. It won acclaim from the totally unsuspecting critics and public alike.

Hope Trueblood was a highly emotional tale of the life and trials of an illegitimate child, set in Victorian England. The *Sheffield Independent* commented favourably: 'Patience Worth must command a wide field of readers by the sheer excellence of *Hope Trueblood*, which contains sufficient high-grade characters, splendidly fashioned, to stock half a dozen novels.' The *Yorkshire Post*, a little more ambiguously, remarked that 'the writer, whose first work this is, harks back to the time in which the Brontës wrote, in order to portray in a form so exactly

Opposite: Mrs Pearl Curran, Patience Worth's amanuensis, who died in 1938. Though 'Patience's' books won critical acclaim, Mrs Curran's own literary abilities were negligible and her education limited. (She thought Tennyson's famous poem was called *The lady of Charlotte*, for example.) It seems impossible that Mrs Curran could have deliberately invented the ghostly Patience – but there is no evidence to show that Patience ever existed on Earth as she claimed

appropriate the biography of a brat. . . .'

Patience's epic 'Golden Age' poem *Telka* contained 60,000 words and made astonishingly accurate use of Middle English phraseology. Her book *The sorry tale* told in 325,000 words the story of a contemporary of Christ whose life ran parallel to his and who ended by being crucified beside him as one of the thieves. *The sorry tale* was written extremely rapidly – in an evening's work of only two hours, Patience Worth could produce an average of 3000 words. In addition, no research was necessary. The details of social, domestic and political life in ancient Palestine and Rome, and the language and customs of Greeks, Arabians, Romans and several sects of Jews are rich and convincing. They could have been set down only by a highly knowledgeable scholar who had specialised in the history of the Middle East of 2000 years ago.

This could not have been Mrs Curran. She had been to Sunday School and that was the limit of her knowledge of the Bible lands.

Lavendar and lace

A purple sky; twilight,
Silver-fringed of tremorous stars;
Cloud rifts, tattered, as old lace,
And a shuttling moon – wan-faced,
  seeking.

Twilight, and garden shadows;
The liquid note of some late songster;
And the scent of lavender and rue,
Like memory of the day aclinging!

PATIENCE WORTH, 12 January 1926

(*'Lavendar' was Patience's own spelling*)

She was not fond of reading and had finished her school education at about 15 years of age. She had never been abroad and, indeed, had rarely left St Louis. Until the appearance of Patience Worth she had concentrated her energies on being a housewife and an amateur singer of some talent. She knew little poetry and the verses she composed as an adolescent were no worse – but certainly no better – than those of any other girl of her age and background. One such work, entitled *The secret tear*, was written when she was 15. It began (with her own spelling reproduced):

I heard a voice whisper 'go out and pray'
See how in the garden the fairies did play
So out I went in the fresh summer air
I spied a sweet rose and she was
  passingley fair
But she hung her fair head, and her
  bright carmean cheek
Could not have been equaled so far as
  you'de seek

This is not the sort of juvenilia one would expect from the pen that was later to 'write' works described by the psychical researcher

Henry Holt as 'very close to masterpieces'. One might make out a case for Mrs Curran being a late developer but this seems unlikely in view of the sheer volume of literature produced through her that was of better than passable quality.

Naturally enough, 'Patience Worth' was intensively investigated by psychical researchers as well as academics. In 1929 Walter Franklin Prince, the Executive Research Officer of the Boston Society for Psychical Research, wrote a book, *The case of Patience Worth*, in which he detailed the investigations to which Mrs Curran had been subjected.

Prince, together with Charles E. Cory of Washington University, one Caspar S. Yost and other members of the Society, searched Mrs Curran's house for books of esoteric knowledge that could have been incorporated, consciously or unconsciously, into such works as *The sorry tale*. They found none. They also noted that the few books of poetry in the Currans' meagre library were unthumbed, and in one the pages were uncut. (Mrs Curran firmly believed that Tennyson's famous poem *The lady of Shalott* was called *The lady of Charlotte*.)

The investigators tested Mrs Curran's ability to write in her own persona by asking her to produce short stories and poetry. These reveal a style that might be expected from a housewife unused to putting her thoughts on paper. Her personality shows through sufficiently to make any connection with the serious Quaker attitudes of Patience Worth seem positively ridiculous.

Other incidents concerning communications from Patience reveal significant gaps in Mrs Curran's education and reading. For

Above: a ouija board in action. This is similar to the one used, at first out of idle curiosity, by Mrs Curran in 1913. The letters of the alphabet, the numbers 1 to 10, and the words 'yes' and 'no' are inscribed on the board. The pointer is mounted on castors and one or more of the 'sitters' places a hand lightly on it. Questions are asked of the 'spirits' and almost every time the pointer moves – as if directed by an invisible force – and spells out messages. Although proper ouija boards are not much used these days, many people use an impromptu version with the letters, numbers and words on pieces of paper arranged in a circle on a table, and with an upturned glass acting as the pointer

The poet from the shadows

A phantom? Weel enough,
Prove thee thyself to me!
I say, behold, here I be,
Buskins, kirtle, cap and petty-skirts,
And much tongue!
Weel, what hast thou to prove thee?
This was Patience Worth's verse entitled 'Patience Worth', a wry comment on her unique status as the genius of the ouija board – the 'phantom' behind the poetry, plays and novels written through Mrs Curran which won major critical acclaim on both sides of the Atlantic.

Among numerous literary works she produced poems, plays and *The sorry tale* – an enormous novel of 300,000 words 'dictated' every evening over a two year period. This massive work (concerning the fate of another child born in Bethlehem on the same night as Jesus) revealed scholarly knowledge of Biblical lands and customs way above

that of the medium. Professors of literature, poets, journalists and churchmen hailed the work as 'the Gospel according to Patience Worth', and gushingly complimented its ghostly author on its brilliance. But not everyone agreed. Some reviewers commented that they found her writing to be 'feverish, high-flown and terribly prolix'. Other reviewers compromised uneasily: 'but it is a wonderful book, well worth wrestling with, and the marvel is, who wrote it?'

For many people the mystery of its authorship was the book's main attraction, while others were prejudiced against it for the same reason, thinking it 'spooky' and distasteful. But Patience Worth – whoever she was – was compared to the Brontës, Keats, Browning, Milton and even Shakespeare. She was often invited to literary receptions, but sent her regrets.

example, a Roman Catholic archbishop in the St Louis area had been preaching that if spirits returned after death, they were 'emissaries of the Evil One'. Mrs Curran asked Patience her views on the subject:

At once Patience had this to say: 'I say me, who became apparent before the Maid? Who became a vision before Bernadette? No less than the Mother; yet they have lifted up their voices saying the dead are in his [the devil's] keeping.' This last about the dead gave us the clue to what she referred, though we had no idea of what she meant by the rest. Looking up the matter the next day we found that Bernadette Soubirous was the Maid of Lourdes. . . .

Subtle impostor?

A fraud would readily acknowledge the need to look up a reference transmitted by a 'spirit' – ah, the reader would think, Mrs Curran had not even heard of Bernadette of Lourdes. But surely Patience's reference to 'the Maid' was not to 'the Maid of Lourdes' but to *the* Maid – Joan of Arc. Surely two visionary women, not one, were being cited to prove that 'spirits' were not always 'emissaries of the Evil One'. If Mrs Curran pretended to miss this point, she was a very subtle impostor.

But who was Patience Worth? Was she really a Quaker woman who emigrated from her native Dorset 300 years before to die a spinster in America? She has not been traced. But her quaint English has been analysed by linguists and apparently she used perfectly the language and idiom of her place and day. The linguists drew attention to the spelling of certain words that were spoken very differently in the 17th century than they are now. For example, 'boy' was pronounced *bwy*, 'with' and 'give' were *wi* and *gi'e*.

But even assuming that Miss Worth had existed and returned to pour out her literary talent – denied fulfilment in life – to Mrs Curran, how could an uneducated Quaker girl know of the customs of ancient Jewish sects detailed in *The sorry tale*?

Did she perhaps gain this extensive knowledge after her death, at a kind of postmortem university? Some Spiritualists would take this view. Other groups believe such knowledge is plucked from the 'Akashic records' (see page 41): in this case, either by Patience Worth, by Mrs Curran's subconscious mind or – who knows? – by both.

Celebrity brought recognition from public bodies. The States Capitol Commission of Missouri, which wished to decorate the walls of the new State House with inscriptions by local literary figures, called on Patience Worth, through Mrs Curran, to supply a short piece. It was to be no more than 120 letters long. Patience immediately produced, as fast as Mrs Curran could write:

'Tis the grain of God that be within thy hands. Cast nay grain awhither. Even

A daughter of the dead

If Patience had been a frustrated writer she remedied that easily through Mrs Curran. But her maternal instinct had also been frustrated, so Mrs Curran received her most bizarre instructions: that she should adopt a baby girl whom she would 'share' with the long-dead Patience. Patience gave Mrs Curran a description of this as yet unborn child: it must have red hair, blue eyes and be of Anglo-Scottish descent.

The Currans found a recently widowed pregnant woman who agreed that they could adopt her child if she happened to die in childbirth. She did indeed die and the child – fitting Patience's description exactly – became known as Patience Worth Wee Curran.

The child grew up, supervised by the ghostly Patience (who insisted on her wearing quaint Quaker-girl clothes) and later moved to California where she married twice. In 1938 Mrs Curran died and Patience fell silent forever. But in 1943, at the age of 27 and in good health, Patience Wee had a premonition of her approaching death. She began to lose weight and a very mild heart ailment was diagnosed. Then, just before Christmas, 1943, she died in her sleep. Many believed that her ghostly 'mother' had come for her own.

Above: Dr Walter Franklin Prince (1863–1934) an ex-Methodist minister and psychical researcher. He was particularly interested in the case of Patience Worth, believing it to be one of the most important psychic case histories of all time

the chaff is His, and the dust thy brother's.

Counting spaces, punctuation marks and letters, this adds up to 120 characters precisely.

The ouija board was soon found to be too slow and clumsy as a means for taking down Patience's dictation. Mrs Curran began automatic writing proper. This involves resting a pen or pencil, held lightly in the hand, on a piece of paper. If one is so gifted, the pen will begin to write of its own accord. But soon even this method became too restrictive for the prolific outpourings of Patience Worth, who began instead to communicate directly with Mrs Curran's mind. She 'spoke' her poetry through Mrs Curran, who at the same time witnessed beautiful, atmospheric visions. Mr Curran took down Mrs Curran's/Patience Worth's utterances in longhand, and they were then typed.

Patience admitted to having burning literary ambition – and also acknowledged that in some way she might be a messenger of God. Perhaps she was suggesting that the mysterious phenomenon she was causing could guide people to God and a belief in eternal things. She wrote: 'I weave not, nay but neath these hands shall such a word set up, that Earth shall burn with wonder.'

The art of automatic writing

Only very rarely does automatic writing produce anything like literature. When a genius of Shakespeare's stature 'comes through', the results are bound to be fascinating.

AUTOMATIC WRITING is still a matter of intense interest among psychologists and parapsychologists alike. Not all occurrences of automatic script are as difficult to explain away as the remarkable case of Patience Worth (see page 48). A leading British psychical researcher and scientist, Professor Arthur Ellison, has said: 'I expect a third of the population of England could produce some form of automatic writing – but the results would be mostly gibberish.'

Anyone can try an experiment by resting a pen lightly on a blank page, diverting their attention from it and letting the pen do what it will. It used to be assumed that automatic script must be the product of discarnate entities, desperate to communicate and grateful for the opportunity to take command of a pen. The only question in believers' minds was: 'Is the communicator an Earth-bound spirit or a spirit sent by God?' But the scribbles produced in automatic writing can reveal a great deal, if not about the spirit world, then certainly about the subconscious mind of the pen-holder.

In the first three decades of the 20th century automatic writing was in fact used as a tool in diagnosing and treating mental

Above: William Shakespeare and his contemporaries. In 1947 a medium named Hester Dowden allegedly communicated with Shakespeare (seated centre) and other Elizabethans through automatic writing. She was told that the plays attributed to Shakespeare were in fact a group effort. Among the contributors were Francis Beaumont (standing third from left), John Fletcher (seated third from left) and Francis Bacon (seated at the end of the table)

disturbances. Dr Anita Mühl was a pioneer of this particular method of encouraging patients to express spontaneously their hidden conflicts.

The beginner in automatic writing may have to be very patient (and suffer writer's cramp before a single word has been written), for it can take hours before the pen begins to move, seemingly of its own accord. Some people never achieve automatic writing; many get meaningless squiggles or jumbles of letters; but a very few get coherent, intelligent and apparently purposeful messages, sometimes in handwriting distinctly different from their own.

An ex-clergyman, William Stainton Moses, was a medium in the latter part of the 19th century who 'specialised' in automatic script, although he could produce these automatisms only while in a self-induced trance. From 1872 to 1883 he filled 24 notebooks with trance-inspired writings, mingled with 'spirit writings', some signed. (Mendelssohn allegedly appended his signature to a page of Moses's script.)

If one takes a sceptical view, certain 19th-century religious works were not directly dictated by angels or by God, as alleged, but were the result of automatic writing by the 'prophets'. *The book of Mormon*, for example, was purportedly dictated by an angel called Moroni to a New York State farm boy, Joseph Smith, in 1827. It was written in a style similar, but inferior, to that of the King James Bible. It is not necessary to believe that Joseph Smith was a liar to doubt that *The book of Mormon* is the word of God.

One early case of automatic writing that is still considered unique is that which involved William T. Stead, a leading British Spiritualist of the late 19th century, and a certain friend who communicated with him automatically through his pen. What is remarkable about this particular case is that the friend was alive at the time. The story goes as follows in Stead's own words:

A friend of mine . . . was to lunch with me on the Wednesday if she had returned to town. On the Monday afternoon I wished to know about this, so taking up my pen I asked the lady mentally if she had returned home. My hand wrote as follows: 'I am sorry to say that I have had the most unpleasant experience, which I am almost ashamed to tell you. I left Haslemere at 2.27 p.m. in a second-class compartment in which there were two women and a man. At Godalming the women got out and I was left alone with the man. He came over and sat by me. I was alarmed and pushed him away. He would not move, however, and tried to kiss me. I was furious and there was a struggle, during which I seized his umbrella and struck him with it repeatedly, but it broke, and I was afraid I would get the worst of it, when the train stopped some distance from Guildford. The man took fright, left me before the train reached the station, jumped out and took to his heels. I was extremely agitated, but I kept the umbrella.'

Stead dashed off a sympathetic note to the lady, explaining the reasons for his solicitude, and – being a thorough investigator – asked her to call, bringing with her the broken umbrella as evidence. She replied in some perturbation, saying she had intended

Above: American psychical researcher Dr J.B. Rhine, who believed that most automatic writings can be explained as the spontaneous expression of subconscious conflicts

Below left: William Stainton Moses, a 19th-century medium who claimed to have received numerous messages from the spirit world through automatic writing. One of his scripts (below), dated 1874, was 'signed' by Mendelssohn – who died in 1847

Below right: Edward de Vere, 17th Earl of Oxford. According to medium Hester Dowden, Oxford wrote the lyrical and romantic passages of 'Shakespeare's' plays, and was the author of most of the sonnets

never to mention the incident to anyone. However, she added, one point in his account of her misadventure was wrong – the umbrella was hers, not her assailant's.

A great American psychical researcher of modern times, Dr J. B. Rhine, was inclined to dismiss automatic writings as spontaneous 'motor automatisms' or, as previously hinted, the outward expression of subconscious conflicts, obsessions or repressions. There seems little doubt that he and his like-minded colleagues are right in this appraisal of much automatic writing. But Dr Rhine admitted that some cases – that of Patience Worth, for example – are not so easily dismissed.

A provocative case of automatic writing occurred in 1947, through the mediumship of Hester Dowden, who had for many years been famous for the automatic scripts that she produced, even when blindfolded. Percy Allen, an author, sat with her while she held written 'conversations', allegedly with Elizabethan dramatists. As a result of these seances Mr Allen believed he discovered the answer to the tantalising question 'Who was Shakespeare?' Was he really Francis Bacon? Lord Oxford? Or perhaps was William Shakespeare just William Shakespeare?

Mrs Dowden claimed she received written information on the matter from those three gentlemen, and also from other Elizabethans involved in the writing or staging of plays. Mrs Dowden's communicators explained that the 'Shakespeare' plays were a group effort. Shakespeare and Lord Oxford were the principal contributors, while Beaumont and Fletcher, famous as the authors of many other plays, occasionally provided additional material. Bacon acted as a kind of stern script editor.

Each did what he was good at: Shakespeare created many of the stronger characters, both comic and tragic, such as Iago and Falstaff,

and he had a talent for dramatic construction, which the others willingly used. Lord Oxford, on the other hand, created the 'honeyed Shakespeare' by writing the lyrical and romantic passages.

Mrs Dowden was similarly informed that it was Lord Oxford who penned the majority of the sonnets. He also 'dictated' three new ones to her.

Bacon reiterated time and again to Mrs Dowden that the body of literature that the world knows as Shakespeare's was a group effort. Will of Stratford himself allegedly told Mrs Dowden:

I was quick at knowing what would be effective on stage. I would find a plot (*Hamlet* was one), consult with Oxford, and form a skeleton edifice, which he would furnish and people, as befitted the subject . . . I was the *skeleton* of the body that wrote the plays. The flesh and blood was *not* mine, but I was *always* in the production.

Of course, automatic literature may be a dramatisation of a deep or repressed creativity, finding expression through a means we can so far only guess at. After all, many writers and artists over the centuries have 'listened' to their 'muse'. Often whole plots, scenes or minutely observed characters have 'come unbidden' to writers, dramatists, poets. Often, when Charles Dickens was dozing in his armchair, a wealth of characters would appear before him 'as it were, begging to be set down on paper'. Samuel Taylor Coleridge dreamed the whole of his poem *Kubla Khan* and would have written it all down for posterity had not someone known to history only as 'a person from Porlock' called casually and put most of it out of his mind forever. Mary Shelley dreamed *Frankenstein*, Robert Louis Stevenson came to rely on his dreams for his stories, including

Above: a 19th-century engraving entitled 'Charles Dickens's legacy to England'. Dickens said that many of his characters simply appeared before him while he was dozing, almost as if they had a life of their own

Left: Mary Wollstonecraft Shelley (1797-1851), creator of *Frankenstein*, one of the most famous 'horror' stories. The plot of the novel came to her in a dream

the allegorical Dr Jekyll and Mr Hyde. When such a writer as Charles Dickens says a tale 'wrote itself', however, we can only assume he did *not* mean his pen shot across the paper inscribing, of its own accord, *Oliver Twist*. Inspiration is in practice very different from the process of automatic writing.

Somewhere between the two, perhaps, lay the strange case of Patrick Branwell Brontë. He was an unfortunate and unsympathetic character, famous mainly for his inability to hold liquor and laudanum, or to cope with sharing an isolated house on the moors with his eccentric sisters Charlotte, Emily and Anne. He had literary pretensions, which came to nothing. However, during one of his brief periods of humble employment (as a railway clerk) he discovered that he could compile the week's railway accounts with one hand, while his other, quite independently, began to scrawl. First the name of his beloved dead sister, Maria, appeared; then came other fragments – some prose, some poetry. He later claimed to have written an alternative version of *Wuthering Heights* by pure coincidence at the same time as Emily was writing a book of the same name.

However, this was the second version of the incident. He had previously stolen the opening chapter of Emily's book and read it to his cronies as his own work. It was only when he was disbelieved that he came up with the 'alternative version' account.

Literature of the dead

Can novels, poems and plays be 'written' by the dead? This chapter describes some notable cases of automatic writing

THERE APPEAR TO BE fashions in paranormal phenomena as in other aspects of life, and automatic writing seemed to have fallen from grace for a period, whether as an attempt to communicate with the dead or even as a party trick. Yet automatic scripts are being produced in vast quantities today. Possibly the world's most important and prolific psychic writer has largely escaped attention in Europe and America because he is a Brazilian, writing in Portuguese that is sometimes extremely erudite and technical.

Francisco Candido ('Chico') Xavier, now in his seventies, is certainly one of Brazil's most popular figures, devoting his life to

Above: 'Chico' Xavier, Brazil's foremost Spiritist writer, at one of his public automatic writing sessions

Inset: the frontispiece of *Parnassus from beyond the tomb* – allegedly written by no less than 56 dead poets

helping the poor and producing edifying, entertaining and highly profitable best-sellers. He does not accept any money for these books, nor any credit. For, he says, he did not write them – discarnate Brazilian authors did.

For the past 50 years Xavier has spent at least five hours a day letting dead authors write through him. He has often given over his precious spare time for the spirits to use, for until his retirement in 1961 he also had a full-time (but humble) job in local government offices.

Best-sellers from beyond

One of 'his' best-sellers is a volume of poetry called *Parnassus from beyond the tomb*. It contains 259 poems (taking up 421 pages) in markedly differing styles, and is signed by 56 of the leading literary figures of the Portuguese-speaking world – all of whom are dead. The poems deal with many subjects – love, the hypocrisy of the priesthood, the nature of human evolution – and some contain jokes. One is a simple declaration of the poet's identity, entitled *Ego sum* (Latin for 'I am'). Translated by Guy Lyon Playfair, author of *The flying cow* and expert on Brazilian Spiritism, it reads: 'I am who I am. Therefore it would be extremely unjust if I did not declare myself; if I lied, or deceived you in anonymity, since I am Augusto.' And the poem is signed 'Augusto dos Anjos', a famous deceased Brazilian poet.

But nothing so far described offers anything like proof that the automatic scripts of Chico Xavier are not either conscious or unconscious frauds (although one would think a conscious impostor would eagerly accept the millions of dollars his books have made over the years).

It is true that Xavier is not entirely illiterate – he had an elementary school education (which, as Mr Playfair wryly points out, can be very elementary indeed in Brazil). But the vocabulary he uses is far above the heads of even educated people – he says he often cannot understand a word of it! This applies to the massive work *Nosso lar* (*Our home*), which totals no less than 2459 pages and was purportedly dictated to Xavier by the discarnate doctor Andre Luiz, a pioneer in tropical medicine. It is in fact a novel in nine books with a very simple plot – the hero dies at the beginning of the first book and the subsequent action takes place in the next world ('our home'). This, says Dr Luiz, is not the paradise that the priests tell of, but is much like our life on Earth. 'Death is merely a change of clothing,' he warns and adds that the hereafter is 'the paradise or hell we ourselves have created.' We have a noble purpose, even the humblest of us, says Luiz:

'We are sons of God and heirs to the centuries, conquering values from experience to experience and millennium to millennium.' Reincarnation, we are told, does take place but the rules governing it are much more complex than many living people, even those who believe in it, can guess at.

This massive sequence of novels discourses at great length on a variety of medical and technological subjects, discussing in detail, for example, the fertilisation of the human egg and the slow processes of evolution on Earth. On 2 February 1958 Xavier took down a lengthy passage containing this sort of phraseology:

The existent hiatus, as noted by Hugo de Vries, in the development of mutationism was bridged by the activities of the Servants of Earthly Organogenesis, who submitted the *Leptothrix* family to profound alterations . . .

Hugo de Vries was a Dutch botanist famous for his work on the laws of heredity – a fact not very likely to be taught at a Brazilian elementary school at the beginning of the 20th century. (Once Xavier had complained to Augusto dos Anjos that he couldn't understand what he was 'writing'. 'Look,' came the reply, 'I'm going to write what I can, for your head can't really cope!')

The spirits dictate

By the mid 1970s he had produced 130 books, all bearing on their title page the phrase 'dictated by the spirit of . . .'. More than 400 discarnate authors are said to have written posthumous works through him, and they are certainly selling better, using Xavier as their 'agent', than they did in life. *Our home* alone had sold more than 150,000 copies by late 1980.

One of his more remarkable achievements – which some consider final 'proof' that dead writers are still working through him – was a bizarre incidence of co-authorship, very reminiscent of the case of the 'cross-correspondences' (see page 58). *Evolution in two worlds* was psychically written by Xavier, in the small town of Pedro Leopoldo, a chapter a time – but *alternate* chapters, making no consecutive sense at all – and by Dr Waldo Vieira, who 'wrote' the interim chapters hundreds of miles away. But it was only when Xavier had finished his pile of disjointed and apparently unfinished chapters that his spirit guide told him to contact Dr Vieira. Of course then the whole project made sense. This was the first of 17 books they were to write in this way. As Guy Lyon Playfair points out, frequently one of Dr Vieira's chapters – written without any knowledge of the previous chapter 'written' by Xavier – takes up the story precisely where the other left off.

Now an old and frail man – nearly sightless in one eye – Xavier spends his days helping at the welfare centre 'his' royalties have financed, writing down spirit messages

THE DIVINE ADVENTURE
IONA : BY SUNDOWN SHORES
STUDIES IN SPIRITUAL HISTORY
BY FIONA MACLEOD

LONDON : CHAPMAN AND HALL, LTD.
1900

Second Edition

Top: the Scottish poet and occultist William Sharp, who had a secondary personality known as Fiona Macleod. Both personalities wrote, but quite differently. Their work was published separately, as Sharp had no sense that Macleod's writing was his own

Above: the frontispiece of *The divine adventure* by Fiona Macleod, a mystical work about the Scottish Isle of Iona, published in 1900

for individuals who need advice, signing books, shaking hands, handing out roses, greeting each new face as if he had been anticipating that very meeting with the utmost pleasure. His 'automatic' writing is often done in public, for perhaps three hours at a time, for anyone to watch. (He writes, said an observer, as if his hand were driven by a battery.) He types up his own psychically produced scripts, answers his own letters (usually over 200 a day, many seeking advice or prayers from him, others simply consisting of fan mail), and attends public Spiritist meetings.

He is widely regarded as a saint – even, by some of his followers, as the reincarnation of St Francis of Assisi. But he has his detractors, and his enemies. The Roman Catholic Church in Brazil believes him to be evil, even possessed by the Devil, and one leading Brazilian Jesuit has taken as his mission in life the utter destruction of Chico Xavier's reputation.

Europeans tend to discount even such well-attested cases as this when they occur in distant and exotic places like Brazil. Yet automatic writing flourishes in Europe today. The young British psychic Matthew Manning, although an accomplished automatic writer in the traditional way, has found that 'spirits' have taken it on themselves to do the writing. Notable amongst them is Robert Webbe, who built and lived in the Mannings' Cambridgeshire home in the 17th century and haunted it for some years. Over 300 names and short phrases in differing styles of handwriting have appeared on Matthew Manning's bedroom wall. After each session of spirit graffiti a blunted pencil would be found on his bed, although during the time of the writings no member of the family had been in the room, or even, on many of the occasions, in the house.

In Scotland a publishing company has been set up devoted entirely to the works of a particular spirit writer – or rather, a pair of authors making up a double personality. One half of the double is William Sharp, a Scot and self-styled poet and occultist, who died at Il Castello di Maniace, in Sicily, in 1905, aged 50. Above his grave close to Mount Etna there is an Iona cross, bearing two epitaphs. One says:

Farewell to the known and exhausted Welcome to the unknown and illimitable.

The other, more obscurely says:

Love is more great than we conceive, and Death is the keeper of unknown redemptions. F. M.

So who was 'F.M.'? These are the initials of Fiona Macleod, his *alter ego*, his feminine side personified, whose name and works had inspired the 'Celtic renaissance' in late 19th-century Scotland.

The Paisley project

Dual, or even multiple, personalities are not unknown in the annals of psychiatric medicine. But what is so significant about 'Wilfion' (Sharp's own collective name for his two selves) is that he/she is allegedly communicating thoughts and poetic works from beyond the grave.

From the early days of 1970 an American expert on William Sharp, Konrad Hopkins, began to receive psychic scripts from many discarnate souls – including one 'George Windsor', better known perhaps as King George VI – but mainly from Sharp himself. In 1974 Hopkins met a Dutch sensitive called Ronald van Roekel and shortly afterwards they began a publishing venture in Paisley, Scotland, called Wilfion Books.

Meanwhile in Ventnor, Isle of Wight, a lady called Margo Williams was discovering her long-hidden gifts as a medium. By summer 1980 Margo had received more than 4000 psychic scripts, purporting to be dictated by more than 360 discarnate persons. The first was her spirit guide, Jane, and the second was someone called William Sharp.

The deceased Scottish poet clairaudiently informed Konrad Hopkins of the Margo Williams connection. A correspondence between the medium and the directors of Wilfion books sprang up and soon arrangements were under way for *The Wilfion scripts* – the Wilfion writings received through Mrs Williams – to be published in Paisley.

There are 92 verses and some prose that make up *The Wilfion scripts*. The verses are, on the whole, short, childish (some would say child-like) and bad. The introduction to the

Above: King George VI, who, as 'George Windsor' is said to have communicated post-humously with the American medium Konrad Hopkins. Hopkins was one of the partners who published *The Wilfion scripts*

Above right: Margo Williams, the medium whose many automatic scripts include poems from 'Wilfion'

verses, by Hopkins and van Roekel, includes this curiously obscure apology for the low quality of the poetry:

Sharp . . . admits that the verse is bad because he is trying to reach a confession of a truly horrific sight which he either saw himself or relived through his ability to pick up sensations at stone circles and it then haunted him the rest of his life.

But Mrs Williams generously ascribes Wilfion 'a masterly economy of words'. On 12 December 1976 William Sharp dictated this through her:

Observes scenes from the past Which impress and will last Scenes which survive throughout ages Make interesting reading on pages.

And, perhaps shrewdly summing up the feelings of many of his latest readers, Sharp had this to write on 19 January 1977:

What a joke
I can cloak
Sharp by name
But be same.
Macleod be known by
Until day I die,
Write tales so strange
Over a wide range
Celtic verse
Sounds much worse
From intelligent being
Little folk to be seeing,
What a joke,
Make men choke
With laughter loud
About Macleod.

In the jargon of parapsychology all these bizarre effects could be the products of 'telepathic psychokinesis', 'motor automatisms', 'repressed psychosexual creativity'. But is this not disguising the fact that we just don't know what is behind them?

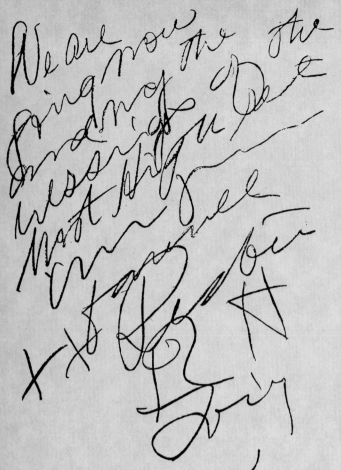

Survival: teasing out the truth

Did a group of dedicated psychical researchers plan – after their deaths – to send evidence of their survival to certain chosen mediums? LYNN PICKNETT describes a controversial series of 'communications'

AN ARDENT AND VOCIFEROUS believer in the afterlife, Frederic Myers, classical scholar and founder member of the Society for Psychical Research (SPR), wished passionately to communicate his belief to others. Judging by an impressive body of evidence, he never desired it more than after his death in 1901. For the following 30 years the SPR collected and collated over 2000 automatic scripts purporting to be transmitted from Myers and other deceased members of the Society through the mediumship of several ladies. They seem to have been specifically designed to prove to the living the reality of the afterlife.

What have become known as the 'cross-correspondences' do indeed indicate that here there was some kind of intelligent communication between the living and the dead – arranged in such a way as to confound critics. Whoever thought it up, on this or the other side of the veil, was very ingenious.

Apart from Myers the purported spirit communicators were Edmund Gurney (died 1888) and Professor Henry Sidgwick (died 1900). The mediums included 'Mrs Holland' (pseudonym of Mrs Alice Fleming), who lived in India and was the sister of Rudyard Kipling; 'Mrs Willett' (pseudonym of Mrs Coombe-Tennant), who lived in London; Mrs A. W. Verrall, a teacher of Classics at Cambridge University; her daughter, Helen (later Mrs W. H. Salter); and the famous trance medium Mrs Leonora Piper, of Boston, Massachusetts.

A bold and complex plan

The purpose and plan of the cross-correspondences are bold yet complex, sometimes almost beyond belief. But it is this complexity that gives them their unique air of authenticity. The plan, as far as it can be understood, is this:

After Myers's death, he and his deceased colleagues from the SPR worked out a system by which fragments of automatic script, meaningless in themselves, would be transmitted through different mediums in widely separated parts of the world. When brought together they would prove to make sense. To make the situation more difficult these fragments would be in Greek or Latin, or contain

Above: Frederic Myers, a respected founder member of Britain's Society for Psychical Research, apparently tried to prove his survival after death to his living friends and colleagues. He supposedly sent messages through various mediums, in widely separated parts of the world, by means of automatic writing, which he had studied intensively in life. The fragment above is in a hand markedly different from the normal script of the medium who produced it, Mrs Leonora Piper

allusions – sometimes fragmentary in themselves – to classical works. In Myers's words as dictated to Mrs Verrall: 'Record the bits and when fitted they will make the whole . . . I will give the words between you neither alone can read but together they will give the clue he wants.'

The erudition of the classical references was beyond the scope of most of the mediums, except the Verralls, showing that the scripts were not the products of their own minds. The fact that the fragments were unintelligible to the mediums themselves would rule out the possibility of joint telepathic composition by them.

It seems that Myers thought of this plan once he had the ultimate personal proof of the afterlife. None of the thoughts he recorded during his earthly life even hints at this scheme. But at least he knew how to set about proving his point: as an ex-president of the SPR he knew which mediums were genuine and competent automatic 'scribes'.

In many cases the various automatists – in England, India and the United States – were instructed to send their apparently meaningless scripts to certain investigators, whose addresses were supplied by the communicators. Each piece of automatic script was to be carefully dated and, if possible, witnessed.

An example of what H. F. Saltmarsh, in *Evidence of personal survival*, calls a 'simple'

Below: Mrs Leonora Piper was one of the most celebrated mediums of modern times. Several of the distinguished researchers who studied her, including Myers, allegedly communicated through her after their deaths

cross-correspondence is as follows. Mrs Piper, in America, heard in a trance state a word she first took to be *sanatos*. She then corrected herself (she was speaking her impressions out loud to be written down) to *tanatos*. That was on 17 April 1907. Later in the month the word came through as *thanatos* and on another occasion was repeated three times. On 7 May the whole phrase 'I want to say *thanatos*' 'came through' Mrs Piper. She did not recognise the word as the Greek for 'death'.

Meanwhile, on 16 April 1907, Mrs Holland in India received a curious opening phrase in her automatic script: 'Maurice Morris Mors. And with that the shadow of death fell on his limbs.' The two names seemed to be an attempt to get to the word *mors* – Latin for death.

The fire of life
Yet again, on 29 April 1907, Mrs Verrall in Cambridge received this cryptic communication: 'Warmed both hands before the fire of life. It fades and I am ready to depart.' Then her hand drew what she took to be the Greek capital letter delta (a triangle). Next came these disjointed phrases: 'Give lilies with full hands [in Latin] . . . Come away, Come away, *Pallida mors* [Latin, meaning 'pale death'].'

There are several allusions to death here:

Hope, star and Browning

Above: Robert Browning, whose poems include *The pied piper of Hamelin*

One of the most famous of the cross-correspondences has been labelled the 'hope, star and Browning' case. In January 1907 one of the communicators (unidentified) proposed – through Mrs Verrall – an experiment: 'An anagram would be better. Tell him that – rats, star, tars and so on . . . .'

A few days later Mrs Verrall received a script beginning:
Aster [Latin for 'star'] *Teras* [Greek, meaning 'wonder' or 'sign'] . . . The very wings of her. A WINGED DESIRE . . . the hope that leaves the earth for the sky – *Abt Vogler* . . .

Mrs Verrall recognised these as fragments from poems of Robert Browning: *Abt Vogler* and *The ring and the book:* Within a week Mrs Verrall's daughter Helen produced an automatic script that included drawings of a bird, star and crescent moon, and verbal references to songbirds.

On 11 February Mrs Piper had a sitting with Mr Piddington. Myers 'came through' and said he had previously communicated something of interest to Mrs Verrall. 'I referred to Hope and Browning . . . I also said Star.'

The investigators noted that 'hope' had been emphasised by the very fact that in the quotation it had been substituted for another word; the quotation should have read 'the passion that left the ground . . .' and not 'the hope that leaves . . . '. Mrs Verrall, who knew her Browning, had remarked after reading through her script, 'I wondered why the silly thing said "hope".'

There was now a clear correspondence between the 'hope, star and Browning' reference of Mrs Piper and the texts of the elder and younger Verrall ladies. Mrs Verrall told her daughter that there had been such a correspondence but, in order not to influence her script, referred not to 'hope, star and Browning' but to 'virtue, Mars (the planet) and Keats'. Two days later Miss Verrall produced another script that included the phrase 'a star above it all rats everywhere in Hamelin town'. This was a clear reference to the poem *The pied piper of Hamelin* – written by Browning.

Frederick Myers had an extensive knowledge of the works of Browning and had always expressed a sympathy with many of his ideals. So perhaps it was natural that his disembodied mind should turn to his old literary favourites when trying to prove his continued existence.

60

Left: A letter from Myers to Sir Oliver Lodge. The automatic scripts allegedly communicated by him were in a different handwriting from this

Below: Mrs A. W. Verrall, key medium in Myers's elaborate post-mortem plan

Above: Mrs Alice Fleming, who was generally known as 'Mrs Holland'. She lived in India at the time the cross-correspondences were being produced

critic has pointed out that the hereafter, judging by the communications of the cross-correspondences, seems to be peopled solely with upper-class Edwardians with a solid classical education and a background of SPR membership. But if the next world were to be more or less a continuation of this one, without the hindrance of physical bodies, then what could be more natural than choosing one's ex-friends and colleagues for an enormous, epoch-making venture? One does not take someone with no head for heights on an Everest expedition.

To suspend disbelief for one moment: it seems that Myers was passionately trying to 'get through', using some means that could actually constitute *proof*. On 12 January 1904 Myers had written (through Mrs Holland in India): 'If it were possible for the soul to die back into earth life again I should die from sheer yearning to reach you to tell you that all that we imagined is not half wonderful enough for the truth . . . .' Through Mrs Piper in the United States he wrote: 'I am trying with all the forces . . . together to prove that I am Myers.' And again, through the Indian connection, he wrote: 'Oh, I am feeble with eagerness – how can I best be identified?'

Sceptical challenges

The whole subject of the cross-correspondences has been analysed and is still the focus of much research. On the evidence of the examples given above there will be many sceptics who will suggest that the whole business was a kind of genteel collusion, perhaps arranged by Myers and his SPR colleagues before their deaths. Or, if conscious fraud seems unlikely, perhaps this series of bizarre word-games was the result of telepathy among the mediums – and the relationship between the two Verrall ladies was surely too close for them to keep secrets from each other. The classical words and allusions came mainly through the mediumship of the women with a classical education – they were almost totally absent in the case of Mrs Willett and Mrs Piper, who did not have this background.

Then there is the fact that the 'Myers' of, say, the Piper scripts, sounds entirely different from that of, say, the Willett scripts. And although the handwriting differed from the women's own hands, it was not actually that of Myers himself.

However, it seemed that Myers and his friends were determined to nip in the bud any such sceptical 'explanations'. In life they had known and challenged both frauds and cynics – they knew what to expect. So, marshalling their spirit forces, they began a barrage of fragmentary and intellectual cross-corresponding communications, spanning continents and decades.

apparently Mrs Verrall had always seen delta as a symbol for death; the 'lilies' quotation is a distortion of a passage in the *Aeneid*, where the early death of Marcellus is foretold; and 'Come away . . .' is from the Shakespearean song in *Twelfth night* that begins: 'Come away, come away, death.' (The first passage, 'Warmed both hands . . .', is a slightly altered quotation from a poem by Walter Savage Landor.)

So three automatists, in three countries and in three languages, received both straightforward and allusive references to the subject of death.

Mr Saltmarsh explains how more complex cross-correspondences might work by giving this hypothetical example:

Suppose that the topic chosen was 'Time'. Automatist A might start the ball rolling by a quotation from the hymn 'Like an ever-rolling stream'. Automatist B might follow on with a quotation from *Alice in Wonderland* dealing with the discussion concerning Time at the Mad Hatter's tea-table, e.g. 'He won't stand beating' or 'We quarrelled last March – just before he went mad, you know' and then, Automatist C gives the clue with 'Time and Tide wait for no man'. . . . Most of the actual cases are far more subtle and it was not until after much research that the connections were discovered. It is probable that even now a good many have been overlooked.

This scholarly jigsaw puzzle may seem at first glance to be a post-mortem game of intellectual snobbery. In fact, more than one

The end of the experiment

Were the cross-correspondences really an ingenious plot designed deliberately to deceive psychical researchers? Or did they, as some would claim, provide the ultimate proof of post-mortem survival?

SINCE THE DEATH in 1901 of F.W.H. Myers, founder member of the Society of Psychical Research, his discarnate spirit – it is widely believed – has communicated many times through the mediumship of living people. In the first quarter of the 20th century the deceased Myers was most active, together with dead friends, in the case of the 'cross-correspondences'.

Over 2000 examples of automatic writing purporting to have come from Myers, Henry Sidgwick, Edmund Gurney and, later, from A.W. Verrall were transmitted through a large number of mediums over a period of 30 years. The scripts took the form of fragmentary literary and classical allusions – clues to a highly complex puzzle, intended by its very erudition to prove the existence of the purported communicators, all of whom had been literary or classical scholars in life. The fragments delivered to various mediums at different times made sense only when taken together, and usually meant little or nothing to the mediums taking them down.

'The sea that moaned in pain'

One of the simpler cross-correspondences was the Roden Noel case. On 7 March 1906 in Cambridge, Mrs Verrall, one of the mediums most heavily used by 'Myers', took down in automatic writing some lines of verse, allegedly from Myers, which began with the words 'Tintagel and the sea that moaned in pain'. The lines meant nothing in particular to Mrs Verrall but her investigator, Miss Johnson of the SPR, thought it reminiscent of a poem by the Cornishman Roden Noel, called *Tintadgel*. Even when Miss Johnson pointed this out to her, Mrs Verrall could not remember having read the poem or even knowing of its existence.

Four days later, in India, Mrs Holland (pseudonym of Rudyard Kipling's sister, Mrs Alice Fleming) received this automatic script: 'This is for A.W. Ask him what the date May 26th, 1894, meant to him – to me – and to F.W.H.M. I do not think they will find it hard to recall, but if so – let them ask Nora.'

The date given is that of the death of Roden Noel. 'A.W.' refers to Dr Verrall and 'F.W.H.M.' to Myers, both of whom were acquainted with Noel. 'Nora' was the widow of Henry Sidgwick, who had been much closer to the poet. But Mrs Holland had not discovered any of these pertinent facts when on 14 March 1906 – one week after the

Henry Sidgwick (below) and Edmund Gurney (below right). Most of the scripts from 'them' containing classical references 'came through' those mediums who had knowledge of Latin and Greek – Mrs Verrall, for example, was a lecturer in Classics at Newnham College, Cambridge (bottom). It may be that the mediums were deliberately chosen because they had such knowledge. Or perhaps the communications stemmed from the mediums' own subconscious minds

English communication, and much too soon to have received any hints from Mrs Verrall or Miss Johnson – she received this script: 'Eighteen, 15, 4, 5, 14. Fourteen, 15, 5, 12. Not to be taken as they stand. See Rev. [the book of Revelation] 13, 18, but only the central eight words, not the whole passage.'

Mrs Holland tried to make sense of the references but found it hopeless. However, when the script was sent to England, Miss Johnson seized the clue of 'the central eight words', which are 'for it is the number of a man'. The numbers cited in the script, when taken as the letters of the alphabet, translate as 'Roden Noel'.

Noel was referred to again in a script from Mrs Holland on 21 March and mentioned in one from Mrs Verrall, in England, on 26 March. On 28 March Mrs Holland's automatic writing included his name spelled out in full with descriptions of his native Cornwall and a muddled description of himself.

A complex case that took years to understand was that of the Medici tombs. It began

in November 1906, through Mrs Holland. Her scripts were full of oblique or unexplained references to evening, morning and dawn, and death, sleep and shadows. In Cambridge on 21 January 1907 Mrs Verrall received the words 'laurel' and 'laurel wreath' repeatedly. Then on 26 February yet another medium, the American Mrs Piper, said out loud (normally she only muttered indistinctly, when coming out of her trances): 'Morehead – laurel for laurel . . . I say I gave her that for laurel. Goodbye.'

Mrs Piper then had a vision of a Negro sitting in place of Mr Piddington, one of the investigators for the SPR, who was with her. She rubbed her hands together and said: 'Dead . . . well, I think it was something about laurel wreaths.' The next day Mrs Piper received: 'I gave Mrs V. laurel wreaths' in her script.

On 17 March Helen Verrall in Cambridge received: 'Alexander's tomb . . . laurel

Above: Mrs Leonora Piper, famous trance medium of Boston, USA, who was involved in a complex case of cross-correspondences that took place between 1906 and 1910. Several mediums 'received' a series of references to shadow, death, sleep, evening, morning, dawn, meditation, Alexander and laurels. Only two years after the last communication did SPR investigators realise that the references pointed to the tombs of the Medici family in Florence. On that of Lorenzo, Duke of Urbino (right), which also contains the body of Alessandro ('Alexander') de Medici, are statues representing Dawn, Twilight and Meditation; the tomb of Giuliano, Duke of Nemours (left) bears figures representing Day and Night. The laurel was an emblem of the Medici family

wreaths, are emblem laurels for the victor's brow.'

Ten days later, in India, Mrs Holland's script included: 'Darkness, light and shadow, Alexander Moor's head.'

A year and a half later, two rarely used mediums – known as 'the Macs' – received: 'Dig a grave among the laurels.'

It was two years before the topic was again referred to by the communicator. This time it was a London medium, Mrs Willett (pseudonym of Mrs Coombe-Tennant), who received: 'Laurentian tombs, Dawn and Twilight.'

A month later, on 8 July 1910, Mrs Piper in the United States spoke the words: 'Meditation, sleeping dead, laurels' when coming out of her trance.

Yet another two years passed before the investigators of the SPR discovered the meaning of the allusions: they referred to the

Above: Helen Verrall (later Mrs W. H. Slater), one of the automatists concerned; she was also a researcher for the SPR

tombs of the Medici family, who were wealthy and powerful in Florence in the 15th and 16th centuries. On the sepulchre of Lorenzo, Duke of Urbino, are statues representing Meditation, Dawn and Twilight. On the tomb of another Medici, Giuliano, are two statues representing Day and Night.

Lorenzo's tomb also holds the body of Alessandro ('Alexander') de Medici, who was murdered; it is, therefore, as much 'Alexander's tomb' as 'Lorenzo's'. Alexander was of mixed blood and in his portraits has clearly Negroid features: truly 'Alexander, Moor's head'.

Helen Verrall had heard of the tombs, but had never visited them and had no detailed knowledge of them. She, like the others, had taken 'Alexander's tomb' to refer to that of Alexander the Great.

But, perhaps significantly, Mrs Holland did know the tombs well. And in one of her previous scripts there were references to Diamond Island, where the new Lodge-Muirhead wireless system was being tested (an experiment in which she was personally very interested). The wireless connection was linked with the tombs references by a striking pun – the fact that one of the wireless pioneers was called Dr Alexander Muirhead (Alexander Moor's head). Yet in the same script was a quotation from *Othello* that reinforced the 'Moor' connection.

So was this witty allusion created by Mrs Holland's subconscious? Knowing the tombs so well, did she perhaps unwittingly make up that particular example of a cross-correspondence? The alternative view is that the communicator deliberately chose mediums whose minds contained relevant material. Communicating through mediums was said to be extremely difficult. The 'Myers' persona had this to say about the problems of communicating from 'the other side' through Mrs Holland:

The nearest simile I can find to express

the difficulty of sending a message – is that I appear to be standing behind a sheet of frosted glass which blurs sight and deadens sound – dictating feebly to a reluctant and somewhat obtuse secretary.

One of those involved in the cross-correspondences was (it seemed) to find out for himself about the reality of the 'frosted glass' simile. On 18 June 1912 Dr A.W. Verrall, husband of Mrs Verrall, died. Six weeks later Mrs Willett received his first post-mortem communication, drawing its allusions from Christina Rossetti, Dante and the humorous magazine *Punch*. His further communications contained family jokes and extremely convoluted classical references. In combination, they proved beyond doubt, according to his 'oldest and dearest friend', the Reverend M.A. Bayfield, that they were from Verrall himself. One of his scripts ends with the wry note: 'This sort of thing is more difficult to do than it looked.'

Fragments and allusions

Most of the 2000 scripts that make up the cross-correspondences are far too complicated to examine here. H.F. Saltmarsh says in his *Evidence of personal survival*:

The fragmentary, enigmatic and allusive nature of these communications is intentional, and their obscurity is due not solely to the deficiencies of the investigators.

Saltmarsh suggested experiments that, while they could not prove the Myers group's post-mortem existence, will demonstrate the difficulties of cheating and of constructing cross-correspondences deliberately.

Begin by choosing a book by an author you know well, and a quotation or subject from it. Then from the same book or another book by the same author pick out a quotation that alludes to the subject without directly mentioning it. Give the two quotations to someone who acts as investigator, and who must try to work out what the connection between them is. It is remarkably difficult, especially if the author's works are unknown to the investigator. Huge leaps in comprehension will have to be made.

When investigating Mrs Willett's 'Myers' scripts, Sir Oliver Lodge remarked:

The way in which these allusions are combined or put together, and their connection with each other indicated, is the striking thing – it seems to me as much beyond the capacity of Mrs Willett as it would be beyond my own capacity. I believe that if the matter is seriously studied, and if Mrs Willett's assertions concerning her conscious knowledge and supraliminal procedure are believed, this will be the opinion of critics also; they will realize, as I do, that we are tapping the reminiscences not of an ordinarily educated person but of a scholar – no matter how

Two of the investigators for the SPR: Eleanor Sidgwick (above), the widow of Henry Sidgwick, and Sir Oliver Lodge (below). The investigators studied each script as it was produced, comparing it with those from other automatists to find any cross-correspondences between them

fragmentary and confused some of the reproductions are.

Saltmarsh's second experiment concerns the improbability that chance could produce cross-correspondences between independent scripts. Simply take a familiar book and open it at random. Eyes shut, point to a passage randomly. Repeat this with another book and attempt to find a cross-correspondence between the extracts.

Despite the impressive weight of scholarly allusions, puns and quotations communicated, many modern psychical researchers regard the cross-correspondences as 'not proven'. Sceptics point out that all the people involved, including the 'investigators', were either members of the SPR or of the same social circle. They could have been in collusion. When reminded that deliberate fraud would have involved cheating on a grand scale (and over 30 years), the sceptics reply that, nevertheless, once begun, it could hardly be exposed.

The clues stop coming

When the last of the SPR's founder-members died, the cross-correspondences stopped, having accumulated to form a huge volume of scripts that any interested party can study at leisure. Cynics want to know why Myers and his group have ceased to communicate their tortuous messages. It may be because there is no one left to receive them, no medium who is – perhaps literally – on their 'wavelength'. Mediumship seems no longer to be practised in classically educated, upper middle-class circles, and there must be few automatic writers who would even recognise Greek characters or apparently nonsensical quotations jumbled together.

It is possible that subconscious telepathy took place among a group of persons, in different parts of the world and over many years. That in itself would be worth investigating. The only other explanation is that there is a life after death – at least for Edwardian gentlemen given to intellectual puns and anagrams – and that, under certain circumstances, the dead may demonstrate their existence to the living.

Although the complex cross-correspondences no longer appear, Myers is apparently still in communication. On 2 April 1972 the young English psychic Matthew Manning received this automatic script, signed 'F. Myers':

You should not really indulge in this unless you know what you are doing. I did a lot of work on automatic writing when I was alive and I could never work it out. No-one alive will ever work out the whole secret of life after death. It pivots on so many things – personality – condition of the mental and physical bodies. Carry on trying though because you could soon be close to the secret. If you find it no-one will believe you anyway.

Knock, knock–who's there?

The strange rappings in the home of the Fox family caused a sensation throughout America – for, as HILARY EVANS explains, many people regarded them as proof that the living could communicate with the dead

WHAT HAPPENED TO Margaretta Fox and her sisters, if it was truly what it purported to be, should have been quite simply the greatest single event in human history. Conclusive proof that we can communicate with the spirits of the dead – which presupposes that the dead exist in spirit form to be communicated with – would mean that thousands of years of speculation were over; death would be positively established as being not the end of life, but a transfer of existence to another and superior plane; our stay on earth could henceforward be regarded confidently, not as a short-lived biological incident, but as part of a continuing process. This, and nothing less than this, seemed to have been established by what occurred in a small wooden house in the village of Hydesville in the state of New York on 31 March 1848. It was this 'breakthrough' that was to mark the beginning of the modern Spiritualist movement, whose adherents were to swell to millions throughout the world in the decades that followed.

There were seven Fox children in all, but only three were actively concerned in the events: Leah, aged 34 in 1848, Margaretta, aged 14, and Catherine, aged 12. The definitive account of the epoch-making incident was supplied by their mother, Margaret, in a

Below right: Catherine Fox who, together with her sister Margaretta (centre right), became the focus for paranormal rappings. These, the girls claimed, said that they had been chosen for the task of convincing the world of a life after death. When the girls travelled to Rochester to stay with their elder sister Leah (far right), the noises travelled with them and even manifested on board the steamer in the course of their journey

Below: the Fox family home in Hydesville, New York state, as depicted in a 1930s postcard. The original building was destroyed by fire; today an exact replica, built in the 1950s, stands on the site

sworn statement four days later, countersigned as accurate by her husband. She told how the house in which they were temporarily living had been disturbed by unaccountable shakings of the walls and furniture, by the sound of footsteps and knockings on the walls and doors. The family had 'concluded that the house must be haunted by some unhappy restless spirit'.

Tired by the disturbances, the family went to bed early on the night of Friday, 31 March. Margaretta and Catherine – the only two children still living with their parents – were frightened by the noises and had left their own room to sleep in another bed in

their parents' room. No doubt it was the reassuring presence of their mother and father that encouraged the girls to respond so cheekily when the sounds recommenced:

> The children heard the rapping and tried to make similar sounds by snapping their fingers. My youngest child, Cathie, said 'Mr Splitfoot, do as I do!', clapping her hands. The sound instantly followed with the same number of raps. When she stopped the sound ceased for a short time. Then Margaretta said, in sport, 'No, do just as I do. Count one, two, three, four,' striking one hand against the other at the same time; and the raps came as before. She was afraid to repeat them. . . .

From this they proceeded gradually to more elaborate questions, using an alphabetical code by means of which it was established

The Fox sisters' parents, Margaret (below) and John (bottom), documented the events of 31 March 1848 – the first day on which the rappings were heard. While they did not believe in 'haunted houses', they came to the conclusion that the noise emanated from a 'restless spirit', which in due course announced that it was a pedlar (above) who had been murdered in the house five years earlier

that the rappings were done by a spirit; eventually the entity identified himself as a pedlar, aged 31, who claimed to have been murdered in that very house, and his remains buried in the cellar.

Neighbours were called in to verify the proceedings; they too heard the raps, put questions of their own and received answers. Next day other visitors came and, in the evening, urged by the spirit, some men started digging in the cellar to see if the story could be substantiated; unfortunately the hole filled with water and the attempt had to be abandoned. Later reports suggest that parts of a body were indeed found, but Mrs Fox does not mention this in her statement of 4 April. She claims that when the noises commenced again on the Saturday evening there were some 300 people present who heard them: there were no noises on Sunday but they began again on Monday and were continuing when she made her statement on the Tuesday.

For the Fox family, then and there, it seemed to be simply a case of haunting. Stories in which the dead return to earth in order to pass messages or warnings to the living have been told throughout history; but in this instance a new element had been added – a two-way conversation between the living and the dead. Others perceived the significance of this and appreciated its implications: as a subsequent historian of the Spiritualist movement, Emma Hardinge Britten, observed, it implied that

> not only the supposed murdered pedlar, but hosts of spirits, good and bad, high and low, could, under certain conditions not understood, and impossible for mortals to comprehend, communicate with earth; that such communication was produced through the forces of spiritual and human magnetism, in chemical affinity; that the varieties of magnetism in different individuals afforded 'medium power' to some, and denied it to others.

Such subtleties were not at first realised, but

it was clear that the Fox sisters were in some way specially gifted to receive these communications: the raps occurred only in their presence, and furthermore occurred wherever they went. When, their lives disrupted by the publicity given to their experiences, the girls and their mother left Hydesville to stay with their sister Leah in Rochester, the rappings travelled with them. And although others were soon to discover that they, too, had some of this 'medium power', the spirits themselves confirmed that the Fox girls were specially endowed. Repeatedly, the messages insisted: 'You have been chosen to go before the world to convince the sceptical of the great truth of immortality.'

Had such messages come out of the blue to young and ignorant schoolgirls in a rural community, it might indeed have been convincing evidence that beings on another plane of existence were seeking to establish communication with us on earth. But the situation was not so simple, for such notions were current in the America of the 1840s.

In the previous century there had been some who considered the newly discovered mesmerism not as an altered mental state that could be accounted for in human terms, but as a process designed to enable communication with the spirits. The controversy had raged ever since. Two years before the happenings at Hydesville, a commentator noted that 'the newspapers and magazines are teeming with slashing discussions upon the subject of magnetism and clairvoyance.'

That commentator was Andrew Jackson Davis, a semi-literate American mystic and psychic, who while in a trance state churned out volume after volume of turgid revelations about life, the Universe, and everything. The fact that his account is full of errors somewhat dents his credibility, but at the time many accepted his heralding of a new era:

It is a truth that spirits commune with

Above: Emma Hardinge Britten, a medium and author of *Modern American Spiritualism* (above right: the title page of the first edition). She helped to establish the new 'religion' in Britain

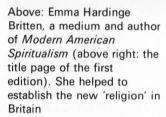

one another while one is in the body and the other in the higher sphere, and this, too, when the person in the body is unconscious of the influx, and hence cannot be convinced of the fact; and this truth will ere long present itself in the form of a living demonstration, and the world will hail with delight the ushering in of that era when the interiors of men will be opened, and the spiritual communication will be established such as is now being enjoyed by the inhabitants of Mars, Jupiter, and Saturn.

Dawn of a new era

Given such utterances, it is not surprising that Davis is often seen as the John the Baptist of the Spiritualist movement. His writings inculcated a mood of expectancy in America, and they explain why the public was so quick to seize on the events at Hydesville as signs of a new age.

Matters advanced with extraordinary rapidity. While staying with their sister Leah at Rochester, the girls were instructed by the spirits to hire the largest hall in the town and give a demonstration of their powers: they did on 14 November 1848. Now at last the whole matter was out in the open; and it was quickly apparent that public opinion was sharply divided between enthusiastic adherents, who had been awaiting just such a revelation, and no less determined sceptics who saw these manifestations as imposture at best, at worst as the work of the Devil. this

Feelings ran frighteningly high. The girls were widely ridiculed, frequently physically attacked: attempts were even made on their lives. When a committee investigated the phenomena and could find no evidence of trickery, its findings were discounted and a second, tougher committee appointed: when this, too, reported that it could detect no imposture, the girls' opponents were only made yet angrier. It became impossible for the Fox sisters to lead normal lives. They left Rochester for Troy, then for the state capital at Albany, and finally for New York, which they reached in June 1850.

The three sisters took New York by storm. The newspaper reporters descended on them, and on the whole treated them kindly; one account admitted:

> We saw none that we could suspect of collusion. . . . We came away utterly disbelieving in all supernatural agency, and at the same time unable to say how any human means could be used without detection.

While it is true that investigative procedures were primitive by present-day standards, it must be accepted that the New Yorkers who sat with the Fox sisters were not eager to be made fools of; hundreds of sitters went determined to be the ones who revealed to the world how the imposture was carried out

– and emerged, if not persuaded that the message of the spirits was genuine, at least that the phenomena defied normal explanation. Horace Greeley, editor of the *Tribune* and one of the most influential men in the country, was persuaded of the girls' integrity and became their valiant champion.

By now other mediums were emerging in emulation of the Fox sisters, but none challenged their pre-eminence. The phenomena developed from rapped questions and answers to automatic writing and spoken utterances, culminating in direct voice communication in which the mediums were 'taken over' by the alleged entities. All kinds of physical phenomena accompanied the messages – movement of furniture, teleportation of objects, levitation of sitters or the medium herself, all kinds of noises and a wide variety of luminous phenomena. Time and time again the sisters were tested, perhaps most strictly when, while visiting England, Kate Fox submitted herself to the

Right: a caricature of Horace Greeley, influential statesman and editor of the *New York Tribune*, from *Vanity Fair* (1872). Greeley gave valuable support to the Fox sisters. He came to believe that the phenomena were genuine, but retained an open mind as to their nature

Below: Andrew Jackson Davis, American mystic and psychic. He had no doubt that it was possible to communicate with the dead (left: an illustration depicting Davis himself receiving information from a 'spirit'), and in the early 1840s he stated that a demonstration of this fact would soon be given. To many Americans, Davis's prediction was fulfilled in 1848, when the Fox sisters' manifestations began, and he was acclaimed as the prophet of Spiritualism

Left: monuments to the Fox sisters and Spiritualism: the obelisk at Rochester (above) where, on 14 November 1848, the girls gave the first public demonstration of their remarkable powers; and the interior of the family home at Hydesville (below), which was turned into a museum

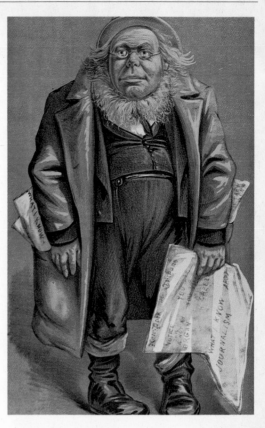

investigations of William Crookes. He vouched for her with persuasive insistence:

> For several months I enjoyed almost unlimited opportunity of testing the various phenomena occurring in the presence of this lady, and I especially examined the phenomena of these sounds. . . . It seems only necessary for her to place her hand on any substance for loud thuds to be heard in it, like a triple pulsation, sometimes loud enough to be heard several rooms off. I have heard . . . these sounds proceeding from the floor, walls, &c., when the medium's hands and feet were held – when she was standing on a chair – when she was suspended in a swing from the ceiling – when she was enclosed in a wire cage – and when she had fallen fainting on a sofa. . . . I have tested them in every way that I could devise, until there has been no escape from the conviction that they were true objective occurrences not produced by trickery or mechanical means.

But not everyone was so thoroughly convinced. From the outset, there had been sceptics who had claimed that the sisters were playing tricks. They had never succeeded in substantiating these claims, and their proposed explanations were generally ridiculously inadequate to account for the phenomena. But their claims were to receive unexpected support, first from the girls' family, then from the mediums themselves.

THE MISSES FOX.

Our readers, believers and non-believers in Spiritualism, will thank us for presenting them portraits of the "original rappers," the Misses Fox, of Rochester, who have made so much noise in the world. The likenesses are from a daguerreotype by Meade Brothers, of New York, and are therefore reliable. Since the origin of the rapping excitement in Rochester, in 1849, mysterious demonstrations of the nature of those of which the Misses Fox were the media have been signalized all over the world; they have given rise to books, pamphlets and newspapers without number, and the believers in their spiritual origin are numbered now by hundreds of thousands. The phenomena exhibited by the media are so curious, that learned and scientific men have felt it their duty to investigate them, and various are the theories by which they are sought to be accounted for. One of the most elaborate works on the subject is that by Professor Mahan. Prof. Faraday, of England, has also given the subject his attention, and honored it with his theory. Congress has been memorialized to appoint a committee of investigation; but as yet our legislators have not seen fit to devote their time to spiritualism. Of the ladies, whose portraits we present, it may be sufficient to remark, that no imposture has been found upon them; and that committees composed of the cutest Yankees, both male and female, have failed to discover any secret machinery or fixtures, by which the sounds heard from and about them might have been produced.

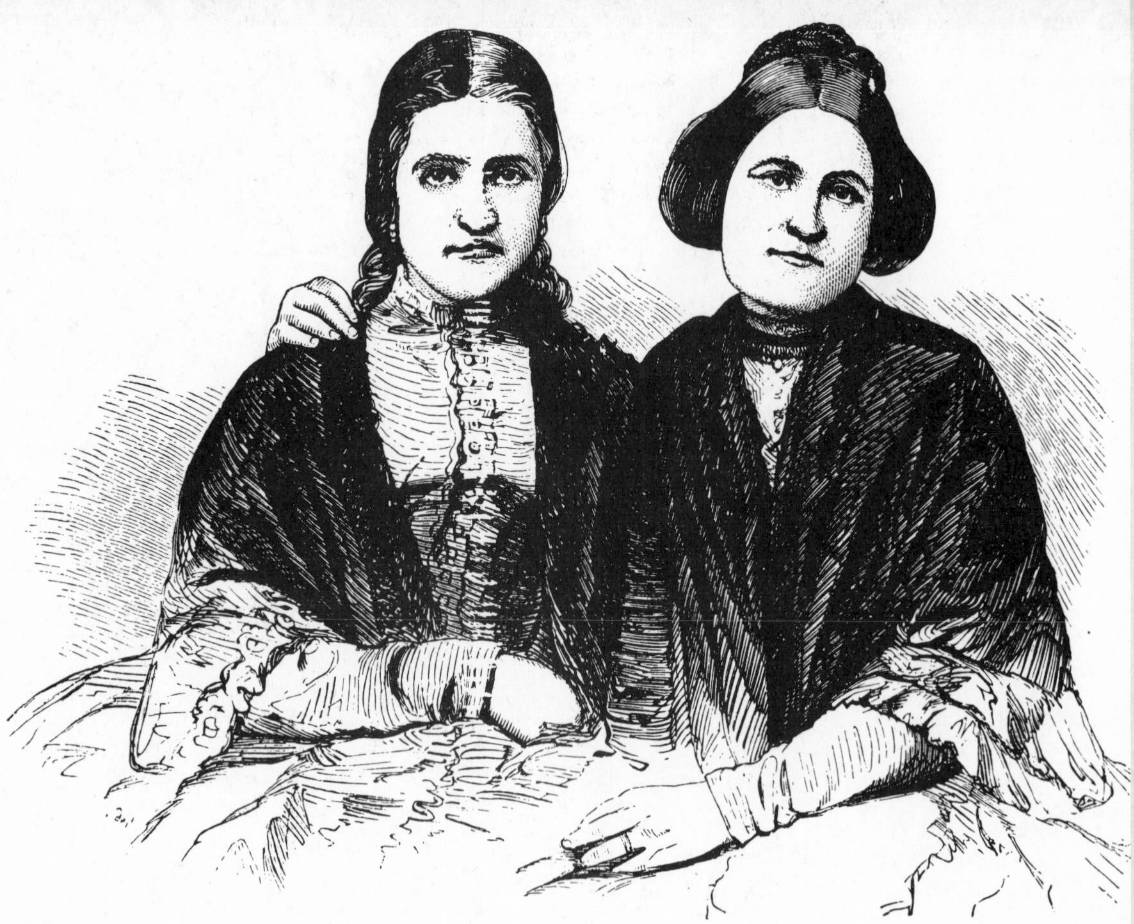

THE SISTERS FOX, THE ORIGINAL SPIRIT RAPPERS.

Confessions and confusions

When the Fox sisters admitted to fraud, the sceptics had a field day. But then the confessions were withdrawn. What is the truth about the acclaimed founders of Spiritualism?

Margaretta and Catherine Fox, the 'discoverers' of Spiritualism. To many, the girls' experiences signalled the dawning of a new era, in which the living could communicate at will with the dead. Others, however, saw the girls simply as clever tricksters and were determined to expose them; but, despite numerous tests and investigations, the sisters were never detected in a hoax

THREE YEARS AFTER the epoch-making events at the Fox family home in Hydesville, USA, on 17 April 1851, a shattering statement was made at Arcadia, New York state, by a Mrs Norman Culver. She was a relative by marriage of the Fox girls, her husband's sister being the wife of their brother David.

She stated that for about two years she had been

> a very sincere believer in the rappings; but something which I saw when I was visiting the girls made me suspect that they were deceiving. I resolved to satisfy myself in some way; and some time afterwards I made a proposition to Catherine to assist her in producing the manifestations.

She claimed that Catherine welcomed her offer, and proceeded to demonstrate how the tricks were worked:

> The raps are produced with the toes. All the toes are used. After nearly a week's practice, with Catherine showing me how, I could produce them perfectly myself. At first it was very hard work to do it. Catherine told me to warm my feet, she said that she sometimes had to warm her feet three or four times in the course of an evening. . . . I have sometimes produced 150 raps in succession.

Such a statement, coming from so authoritative a source, cannot be lightly set aside, particularly as she demonstrated her ability to produce raps. It is impossible for us today to determine what motivated Mrs Culver's revelation. It may have been simple love of the truth, or there may have been some jealousy to inspire the statement. On the face of it, her revelations seem inadequate to account for *all* the phenomena associated with the Fox sisters; but they do show how *some* of them could have been effected. Clearly, trickery cannot be ruled out as a possible partial explanation.

At the same time, it is a fact that the sisters were tested and investigated time and time again, and that never once were they detected in flagrant imposture. As their champion, *Tribune* editor Horace Greeley, pointed out, it was indeed likely that many of their feats could be reproduced by stage magicians, but these were accomplished performers and the girls had none of their skills or training. Greeley was impressed as much by the Fox sisters' failures as by their successes:

A juggler can do nearly as well at one time as another; but I have known the most eminent mediums spend a long evening in trying to evoke the spiritual phenomena, without a gleam of success. I have known this to occur when they were particularly anxious to astound and convince those who were present. . . .

'An absolute falsehood'

But the logic of their defenders and the favourable findings of investigators were forgotten when, on 24 September 1888, Margaretta (now Mrs Kane) told a reporter from the *New York Herald* that she intended to reveal that their mediumship had been a fraud from start to finish. Her younger sister Catherine (now Mrs Jencken) arrived from England to support her. On 21 October a huge crowd gathered in the New York

Although Leah, the eldest of the Fox sisters, had not been involved in the original rappings at Hydesville, she was the first of the three to become a professional medium and, in the 1850s, held many private seances in the parlour of her New York home (right). She also co-operated in a wide variety of experiments, convincing the investigators that the sounds she created had nothing to do with the physical body and that 'the medium has no more power over the sounds than the investigators have'

In 1851 a group of researchers came up with an explanation for the rappings: when the Fox sisters' legs were held, the noises stopped; therefore the girls must be 'popping' their knee joints. Sceptics seized on this as proof of the mediums' deception – but still they could not account for the variety of noises or the levitation of tables that occurred at many of the seances

Academy of Music to hear the confession:
I am here tonight as one of the founders of Spiritualism to denounce it as an absolute falsehood from beginning to end, as the flimsiest of superstitions, the most wicked blasphemy known to the world.

The *New York Herald* described the reaction:
There was a dead silence. Everybody in the great audience knew that they were looking upon the woman who is principally responsible for Spiritualism, its foundress, high-priestess and demonstrator. She stood upon a little pine-table with nothing on her feet but stockings. As she remained motionless loud, distinct rappings were heard, now in the flies, now behind the scenes, now in the gallery . . . Mrs Kane became excited. She clapped her hands, danced about and cried: 'It's a fraud! Spiritualism is a fraud from beginning to end! It's all a trick! There's no truth in it!' A whirlwind of applause followed.

It should have been the death-blow to the movement for whose birth Margaretta had been responsible. But though perhaps a majority of those present were convinced, others were not; and their reservations were justified just over a year later when first Catherine and then Margaretta took back their confessions. Margaretta told a reporter from *The Celestial City*, a New York Spiritualist paper:
Would to God that I could undo the

injustice I did the cause of Spiritualism when, under the strong psychological influence of persons inimical to it, I gave expression to utterances that had no foundation in fact.

She insisted that the charges she had made against Spiritualism had been 'false in every particular'. She refused to say who had put pressure on her, but mentioned that 'persons high in the Catholic Church did their best to have me enter a convent.' She had in fact been converted to the Catholic faith soon after the death of her husband, whom she had married at the age of 16 and lived with only briefly.

She also blamed her sister Leah, accusing her of having drawn Catherine and herself into the career of mediumship. It may well be the case that Leah encouraged her younger sisters, and perhaps, as the most practical and far-sighted of the family, she had taken upon herself the decision to commit the three of them to a course of life that could not but put great social and

Right: the Swedish singer Jenny Lind who, after attending a seance held by the Fox sisters, was convinced that the mediums were genuine

Below: Margaretta's husband, the Arctic explorer Elisha Kent Kane. His letters and verses contained many references to his wife's 'deceit' and implored, 'Do avoid spirits.' After Kane's death in 1857, Margaretta agreed to the publication of this damning evidence, thereby implying that she had – as accused – been guilty of cheating

emotional stress on them all. But never at any previous time had there been any sign that this was resented by her sisters, nor that she was eager where they were reluctant.

What, then, was the truth behind the confessions made and withdrawn? Certainly one fact must be faced: if Margaretta could produce trick raps on the stage in demonstration of her ability to cheat, there is a strong presumption that those tricks had been used in the course of her mediumship – for why otherwise would she have developed the necessary skill?

The suggestion that she cheated, at least some of the time, is confirmed from an unexpected source: her husband. The eminent Arctic explorer Elisha Kent Kane had fallen in love with Margaretta when she was only 13; for three years, against his family's opposition, he courted and helped her, finally marrying her – only to die shortly afterwards, of illness, away from her in Cuba Distracted by grief, Margaretta published the letters and verses he had written to her during those years: they contain abundant evidence that he believed her to cheat. 'Oh Maggie,' he wrote in one letter, 'are you never tired of this weary, weary sameness of continual deceit?' And in another, 'Do avoid "spirits". I cannot bear to think of you as engaged in a course of wickedness and deception.' His verses echo the same sentiments:

Then the maiden sat and wept,
Her hand upon her brow;
So long this secret have I kept,
I can't forswear it now.
It festers in my bosom,
It cankers in my heart,
Thrice cursed is the slave fast chained
To a deceitful art.

The fact that Margaretta allowed such incriminating documents to be published suggests that she was conscious of having used trickery; but if we accept the account she presented in 1888, of total deceit from start to finish, we find ourselves faced with almost as many difficulties as if we accept all as genuine. One of the many eminent sitters with the Fox sisters was the singer Jenny Lind, who perceptively distinguished between the physical and the mental phenomena: 'If it were possible for you to make these sounds, I know it is impossible for you to answer the questions I have had answered this evening.'

Reporters at the ready

Dozens of testimonials survive, recorded at the time by sitters who were convinced – often despite their previous scepticism – of the Fox sisters' psychic ability. If some visitors erred by excessive gullibility, others surely made up for it by implacable scepticism; and at all times there were reporters on hand, eager to seize on anything the least suspicious. All who investigated in hope of exposing the mediums as frauds came away frustrated.

This is not to say that the sisters' manifestations were accepted for what they purported to be. There were many, like Horace Greeley, who admitted the genuineness of the phenomena as phenomena, but retained an open mind as to their nature:

Whatever may be the origin or cause of the 'rappings', the ladies in whose presence they occur do not make them. We tested this thoroughly and to our entire satisfaction. . . . The ladies say they are informed that this is but the beginning of a new era, in which spirits clothed in the flesh are to be more closely and palpably connected with those who have put on immortality; that the manifestations have already appeared in many other families, and are destined to be diffused and rendered clearer, until all who will may communicate freely with their friends who have shuffled off this mortal coil. Of all this we know nothing, and shall guess nothing; but if we were simply to print the questions we asked and the answers we received, during a two-hours uninterrupted conference with the 'rappers', we should be accused of having done so expressly to sustain the theory which regards these manifestations as the utterances of departed spirits.

It seems not merely charitable but reasonable to attribute the 'confessions' of the two younger sisters to the strains of their personal predicament. Both had been schoolgirls when the events started, and throughout the early years; both had been swept from a rural obscurity to a prominent position in one of the world's greatest cities. The tragic end of Margaretta's story-book love affair would have unbalanced a girl far less precariously situated; she took to drink

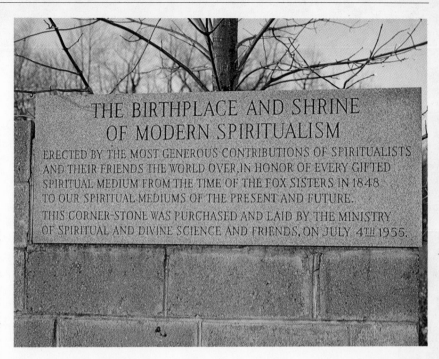

The cornerstone of a shrine to modern Spiritualism, which stands at the rear of the replica of the Fox cottage in Hydesville, USA. The building of the shrine started in 1955, but it was left uncompleted

and drugs, as did her sister Catherine before her own marriage to the lawyer Henry Jencken; though this brought her two children, it was also terminated by his abrupt and early death.

In these circumstances, and perhaps influenced by the enemies of Spiritualism, it would not be surprising if the two sisters, neither of them notably intelligent at the best of times (Crookes was scathing about Catherine's intellectual limitations), reached a state of confusion in which the truth and the falsehood of their careers became inextricably confounded.

In 1904, when all the Fox sisters were dead, a wall of their old home at Hydesville collapsed: among the debris exposed there were found the remains of a body. Whose body it had been, it was impossible to determine: but it is a curious confirmation of the 'messages' that had been given to the Fox sisters half a century before. From this it does not necessarily follow that the information came from the spirit of the dead man, but it would demonstrate that the Fox sisters' careers were, at the very least, founded in truth.

Whether, as time went on and the pressure on them to produce phenomena to order increased, the Fox sisters 'helped out the spirits' by resorting to trickery, must be a matter for individual judgement; the girls were never detected in imposture, and the evidence for it is only circumstantial. But the presumption is there: and it is hard to believe that the Fox sisters could have been induced to make confessions that were totally false, without the least shade of guilt to provide a lever for those who sought to persuade them to confess. In its confusion of truth and falsehood, in its baffling ambiguity, the career of the Fox sisters seems to be a paradigm of Spiritualism itself.

THOMAS ALVA EDISON was one of the greatest practical scientists of the 19th century. His achievements included the perfection of the 'duplex' telegraph, the invention of the phonograph and the introduction into the United States of the first electric light. In 1882 his generating station brought electric street lighting to New York for the first time, and 12 years later his moving picture show, which he called his 'kinetoscope parlour', was opened in the city.

Despite these solid successes, however, an interview he gave to the *Scientific American* in 1920 caused concern among his contemporaries, some of whom must have thought that the 73-year-old inventor had lapsed into senility. What he proposed, in the issue of 30 October, was no less than an instrument for communicating with the dead:

> If our personality survives, then it is strictly logical and scientific to assume that it retains memory, intellect and other faculties and knowledge that we acquire on this earth. Therefore if personality exists after what we call death, it is reasonable to conclude that those who leave this earth would like to communicate with those they have left here. . . I am inclined to believe that our personality hereafter will be able to affect matter. If this reasoning be correct, then, if we can evolve an instrument so delicate as to be affected, or moved, or manipulated . . . by our personality as it survives in the next life, such an instrument, when made available, ought to record something.

Edison worked on the development of such an instrument, but was unsuccessful. However in the opinion of many modern scientific researchers, his views were apparently vindicated in the summer of 1959.

At that time a celebrated Swedish painter, musician and film producer named Friedrich Jürgenson took his battery operated tape recorder out into a remote part of the countryside near his villa in order to record birdsong. Playing the tapes back later, Jürgenson found not only bird sounds but faint human voices, speaking in Swedish and Norwegian and discussing nocturnal birdsong. Despite the 'coincidence' of subject matter, Jürgenson first thought that he had picked up a stray radio transmission. On repeating the experiment, however, he heard further voices, this time addressing him personally and claiming to be dead relatives and friends of his. Over the next few years, working from his home at Mölnbo, near Stockholm, Jürgenson amassed the evidence that he was to present in his book *Voices from the Universe* in 1964. This proved sufficiently convincing to attract the attention of the eminent German psychologist Professor Hans Bender, director of the Government-funded parapsychological research unit at the University of Freiburg, who in turn set up a team of distinguished

The ghosts in the machine

Has the modern tape recorder provided evidence of survival after death? Thousands of voices – purporting to be those of the dead – have been recorded and there is no rational explanation for their origin. What are we to make of them? FRANK SMYTH investigates

Above: Thomas Alva Edison (1847–1931), inventor of the phonograph and the electric light bulb. In 1920 he worked on the development of a device that would, he believed, make possible a form of telepathic contact with the dead

scientists to repeat the experiments and analyse the results.

Their findings can be summarised as follows: that under differing conditions and circumstances a factory-clean tape, run through an ordinary tape-recording head in an otherwise silent environment, will contain human voices speaking recognisable words when played back; that the origin of these voices is apparently inexplicable in the light of present day science; and that the voices themselves are objective in that they yield prints in the same way as normal voices, and register as visible oscillograph impulses on videotape recordings.

The implications of these 'voices from nowhere' are enormous. Dr Bender himself is reported to consider them of more importance to humanity than nuclear physics;

An ordinary cassette tape recorder can be used to record 'electronic voices' but, generally speaking, the better the equipment, the more satisfactory the results. Machines with volume, tone and level controls make the task of deciphering the voices on playback much easier, and a good set of headphones is essential.

Experts agree that the hours between sunset and sunrise are the best time for experiments. Most researchers prefer to work in a quiet room, although a portable tape recorder in a quiet place in the countryside can yield good results, as Jürgenson proved.

Raudive recommended that the date and time should be spoken into the microphone before each session, followed by an invitation to the voices to speak. Each recording session should be no longer than two minutes, as intense concentration is needed in listening to the

Recording the voices yourself

playback of the voices.

Three basic recording methods are most likely to be of use. With the first, the tape recorder is simply switched to 'record', then questions are asked aloud and noted on paper.

With the second method, preliminary announcements are made through a microphone which is then unplugged and a radio attached to the recorder instead. The radio is tuned between frequencies, to a band of 'white noise', and the recording level is set mid-way between maximum and minimum.

The third method involves the use of a diode receiver, a small crystal set that is plugged into the microphone socket of the tape recorder. The recording level is set at maximum. According to Raudive, diode recording gives the best results, the voices being slower, clearer and more natural.

Right: Friedrich Jürgenson (seated), the discoverer of the voice phenomenon, with Professor Hans Bender. Together with a team of scientists, Professor Bender studied the voices received by Jürgenson and conducted exhaustive experiments with his own recordings

at the very least, he concluded in a paper for *Parapsychology Review*, the 'paranormal origin of the phenomena is highly probable.'

Other scientists besides Dr Bender were to become fascinated by Jürgenson's odd discovery. Dr Konstantin Raudive, former professor of psychology at the Universities of Uppsala and Riga, was living in Bad Krozingen, Germany, when he heard of the Jürgenson-Bender experiments in 1965. A former student of Carl Jung, Dr Raudive had been forced to flee from his native Latvia when it was invaded and annexed by the Soviet Union in 1945. Since then he had become well known as a writer on experimental psychology.

Dr Raudive too, began recording tests on the mysterious voices with conspicuous success, and between 1965 and his death in 1974,

in partnership with physicist Dr Alex Schneider of St Gallen, Switzerland, and Theodor Rudolph, a specialist in high frequency electronic engineering, he made over 100,000 tapes under stringent laboratory conditions. An exhaustive analysis of his work was published in Germany in the late 1960s under the title *The inaudible made audible*; this caught the attention of British publisher Colin Smythe, who later brought out an English language edition entitled *Breakthrough*.

Peter Bander, who wrote the preface to the book, later gave an account of how he first heard a strange voice on tape; this nicely illustrates 'what happens' as a rule, and also points out the objective nature of the phenomenon. Colin Smythe had bought a new tape and had followed Dr Raudive's instructions on how to 'contact' the voices. A certain rhythm resembling a human voice had been recorded, but it was unintelligible to Mr Smythe. Peter Bander played the relevant portion of tape over two or three times, and suddenly became aware of what the voice was saying. It was a woman's, and it said *'Mach die Tür mal auf'* – German for 'Open the door'. Mr Bander immediately recognised the voice as that of his dead mother – he had been in the habit of conducting his correspondence with her by tape recording for several years before she died. And the comment was apt: his colleagues often chided him for being unsociable by shutting his office door.

Startled, Mr Bander asked two people who did not speak German to listen to the tape and write down what they heard phonetically. Their versions matched what he had heard exactly: Peter Bander was convinced of the authenticity of the voices.

Since the publication of *Breakthrough* in 1971 serious research has begun in all parts of the world. The interest of two very different bodies reflects the spiritual and temporal

Right: Dr Konstantin Raudive with the 'goniometer', an instrument that was designed for him by Theodor Rudolph of Telefunken to record 'spirit' voices

Below: the Right Reverend Monsignor Stephen O'Connor (right), Vicar General and Principal Roman Catholic Chaplain to the Royal Navy, listening to a voice recorded by Dr Raudive (left). The voice seemed to be that of a young naval officer who had committed suicide two years earlier

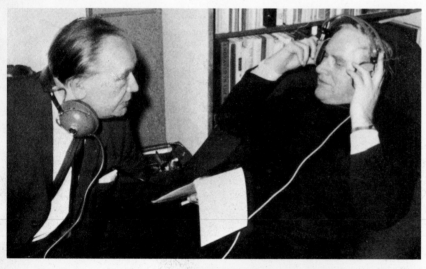

aspects of the voices. The Vatican has shown a great deal of 'off the record' awareness of the phenomena, and a number of distinguished Catholic priest-scientists have conducted experiments of their own. Pre-eminent among the first of these researchers was the late Professor Gebhard Frei, an internationally recognised expert in the fields of depth psychology, parapsychology and anthropology. Dr Frei was the cousin of the late Pope Paul VI, the pontiff who, in 1969, decorated Freidrich Jürgenson with the Commander's Cross of the Order of St Gregory the Great, ostensibly for documentary film work about the Vatican. But Jürgenson told Peter Bander in August 1971 that he had found 'a sympathetic ear for the voice phenomenon in the Vatican'.

The interest of the National Aeronautics and Space Administration (NASA) came to light in the late 1960s when two American engineers from Cape Kennedy visited Dr Raudive at Bad Krozingen. The visitors examined Dr Raudive's experiments minutely, and asked many 'unusually pertinent questions' as well as making helpful comments. They refused, unfortunately, to give the scientist any indication of what relevance the voice phenomena might have to America's space programme. But as Dr Raudive reasoned: if he could achieve clear and regular results on his relatively simple equipment, how much more likely was it that the sophisticated recorders carried in space craft should pick up the voices? From whatever source they spring, Jürgenson's voices from the Universe represent a whole new field in the study of the paranormal.

Right: Pope Paul VI who, in 1969, decorated Friedrich Jürgenson with the Commander's Cross of the Order of St Gregory the Great. The Catholic Church has never expressed an official opinion on the nature of the mysterious voices, but Jürgenson has said that he found 'a sympathetic ear' for the phenomenon in the Vatican

Whispers of immortality

How can we explain the mysterious voices that appear on tape from no apparent material source? Can they truly be the voices of the surviving dead as many people believe or do they somehow emanate from those present at the recording sessions?

WHEN FRIEDRICH JÜRGENSON taped his first mysterious voices in 1959, he was using an ordinary portable reel to reel tape recorder with a microphone attached to the instrument by a lead. Subsequent researchers have used two other basic methods with great success: the radio and the diode. In the former, an ordinary radio is attached to the tape recorder's microphone socket and tuned to a point between stations that produces rushing sounds, known as 'white noise'. In the latter a diode – a rectifying device that allows current to pass in one direction only – is plugged into the microphone socket. The diode used by Konstantin Raudive was an ordinary crystal set – the 'cat's whisker' of early radio days. From a technical point of view the aerial used with his diode was only a couple of inches long – totally impractical for receiving any clear 'normal' radio signal.

While these simple techniques have provided results quite sufficient to convince most amateur researchers, it was obvious from the outset that the world of science would require much more sophisticated tests

Below: the first of the two controlled experiments set up in 1971 by Colin Smythe, under the supervision of Pye Records Ltd, before committing his company to publishing Dr Raudive's book *Breakthrough* in the English language. Among those present were (from left to right): Dr Raudive, Peter Bander (a director of Colin Smythe Ltd and author of the preface to *Breakthrough*), Ken Attwood and Ray Prickett (Pye's chief recording engineers) and Sir Robert Mayer (chairman of Colin Smythe Ltd). Over 200 voices appeared on the tape during the 18 minute recording session

before admitting that the paranormal might be behind Jürgenson's curious phenomena.

Accordingly, in 1971 Colin Smythe set up two carefully controlled experiments before committing his company to publishing Konstantin Raudive's book in English. The first of these was on 24 March at Gerrard's Cross, Buckinghamshire, under the supervision of Pye Records Ltd and the company's two chief recording engineers, Ray Prickett and Kenneth Attwood.

All the equipment was provided by Pye, and included instruments to block out freak pick-ups from radio stations and high and low frequency transmitters, as well as specially protected tapes. A bank of four tape recorders was synchronised so that one recording was made through a microphone, giving a true account of any normal noises in the room, and a sophisticated diode was also fitted, with a recording indicator attached. The audience, which included Dr Raudive, Colin Smythe, Peter Bander and the chairman of Colin Smythe Ltd, Sir Robert Mayer, was assured by the two engineers that this machinery should render any recording through the diode impossible.

The tapes rolled for 18 minutes, during which time the recording indicator attached to the diode flickered constantly, although Ray Prickett, monitoring on headphones, could hear nothing. The playback, said Mr

Prickett, was 'astounding'. Over 200 voices appeared on the tape, 27 of which were so clear that they were intelligible to everyone present. Sir Robert Mayer in particular was startled to recognise the voice of his old friend the late Artur Schnabel, a celebrated concert pianist. An unidentified voice referred to Dr Raudive as 'Kosti' – his childhood nickname.

The second experiment was conducted three days later on 27 March, at the Enfield laboratories of Belling & Lee, using a radio-frequency screen laboratory that excludes any type of electromagnetic radiation. The experiment was supervised by Peter Hale, Britain's leading expert in electronic screen suppression; he was assisted by Ralph Lovelock, a top physicist and electronics engineer. Again, clear voices appeared on the screened-off tapes.

Peter Hale's response was frank. 'The result of last Friday's experiment . . . is such that I cannot explain it in normal physical terms,' he wrote to Colin Smythe. Ralph Lovelock concurred with this view.

So the objective reality of the voices – whatever their cause – was established to the satisfaction of highly respectable scientists. But what was the nature of the voices? What sort of thing did they say?

Most experimenters report that the voices speak in a curious rhythm, at first alien to the ear. But once the listener has picked up the 'tempo', the phrases and short sentences become readily understandable. The voices speak as if they are racing against time, as if, as one researcher put it, 'either their time "on the air" is limited, or their energy is giving out.' The actual language used seems to depend upon the native tongue of the person to whom the message is addressed: both Peter Bander and Sir Robert Mayer had German origins, and the voices spoke to them in German. Dr Raudive was multi-lingual, and when he was present the voices often used several languages.

'The sentence construction', Raudive explained, 'obeys rules that differ radically from those of ordinary speech and, although the voices seem to speak in the same way as we do, the anatomy of their "speech apparatus" must be different from our own.'

Dr Raudive, like Jürgenson, was a devout Catholic, and it was perhaps natural that his prime interest should be in establishing that the voices were truly those of the surviving dead. He evolved a system of communicating with them, a kind of electronic 'ouija' or 'table-turning' technique, asking questions aloud and inviting the 'spirits' to reply. Unfortunately the answers were short and rarely very informative. Repeatedly, the voices appeared to avoid direct questions and insisted on being taken at 'face value'. 'Please believe; I am.' 'We are.' 'The dead live.' 'I am alive Konstantin.'

A note of surprise is often detected in the voices as they 'come through', almost as if the

Above: the late Artur Schnabel, composer and concert pianist, who was a close friend of Sir Robert Mayer. When listening to the playback of the recording made during the Pye experiment, Sir Robert was astonished to hear Schnabel's voice on the tape. As a result of the experiment, Sir Robert agreed to go ahead with the publication of Dr Raudive's book. He said: 'If the chief engineers of Pye are baffled, I don't see why we should not present this remarkable discovery to the general public'

earthly attempt to contact them has aroused them from some sort of daze. Reporter Harald Bergestam investigated the state of Swedish research for *Fate* magazine's March 1973 issue. He wrote: 'We heard a man's voice saying clearly "I am living" and he repeated this. The second time his voice was filled with excitement and happiness. We understood that he had just come to realise that although he had died he still lived.'

To the Catholic Dr Raudive, the most important messages seemed to confirm both the existence of Christ and the Church's doctrine of purgatory. Many voices asked for prayers, and assured the experimenter that they could be helped by prayer. Others said: 'Jesus wandered here in loneliness.' 'Here is Christ, here are the priests.' One voice asked: 'Great Lord, remember Raudive!'

When Dr Raudive asked if the speakers could communicate through the tape recorder at will, one voice replied: 'On the Heavenly Father; the will of man is limited.'

On the other hand some messages appear to refer to the Devil, saying: 'Pray! I am in the power of the evil one.' 'The devil exists.'

Puzzlingly, a number of voices express earthly concerns, asking for cigarettes and drink, talking of the 'officialdom' that exists on their plane, and commenting on the clothing of the experimenters – perhaps an indication that they can 'see' as well as speak to their interlocutors.

When the living intrude

An interesting sequence was recorded during an experiment conducted by Friedrich Jürgenson with Professor Hans Bender in July 1971. Jürgenson was at home awaiting the arrival of Professor Bender and his team, which included a girl named Gisela. He had been recording, and when he played back the tape a German voice said: '*Sie kommen bald. Zahnarzt. Zahnarzt.*' ('They will come soon. Dentist. Dentist.')

When the Bender group arrived, Jürgenson was told that Gisela had suffered severe toothache at about the time he had recorded the voice. As it chanced, Jürgenson's wife was a dentist, and arrangements were made for Gisela to attend her surgery while the group continued with their experiments. Some time later, a woman's voice on the tape said '*Peng!*' – a German interjection used like 'Bingo!' to show that something has been accomplished. The voice sounded like that of Gisela and came through at just the time when Gisela's tooth was being extracted.

The incidents surrounding Gisela's toothache closely resemble the phenomenon known to psychical researchers as a crisis apparition. Expressed simply, a crisis apparition occurs when one person, the 'receiver', suddenly becomes aware that another person, the 'transmitter', is undergoing a crisis – pain, shock, emotion – even though the 'transmitter' is some distance away. The most common examples of such phenomena

he was the only person in the room who knew the name.

To agnostic parapsychologists, the theory of TPK is perhaps more acceptable than the 'voices from the dead' alternative, and may explain such discrepancies as the inconsequential nature of some of the phrases recorded: odd words and half-wrought phrases form and dissolve continually in the subconscious mind, after all, and might be projected onto tape if involuntary TPK is involved.

But even granting TPK as the explanation, could not Edison and Raudive still be correct? May not the surviving dead be able to use such preternatural ability with conscious direction?

As holder of the Perrot-Warwick postgraduate studentship for psychical research at Trinity College, Cambridge, David Ellis

Russian author Valery Tarsis was present at one of Dr Raudive's recording sessions in 1967 when the voice of his old friend Boris Pasternak (above), author of *Dr Zhivago*, 'came through'. Pasternak, who died in 1960, commented on Tarsis's escape from the Soviet Union in 1966, on the book Tarsis was then working on, and on Pasternak's friend Olga. Perhaps both Tarsis and Pasternak could derive comfort from the fact that one of their old tormentors, Joseph Stalin (right), appeared to be getting his just deserts on the 'other side': another of Dr Raudive's tapes yields the words: 'Stalin. Terribly hot here'

occur in times of war, when a mother, for instance, may report seeing or hearing her son at the moment he is wounded – often at the moment of his death. The theory is that the pain and shock trigger off involuntary telepathic contact between son and mother. If Gisela's pain was sharp enough, and the relief of the pain intense enough, she may have projected her emotions telepathically; but for those emotions to affect a machine another factor would have to be involved: psychokinesis, known as PK.

PK is the affecting of physical objects through 'the power of the mind' alone. If telepathy was responsible for Gisela's voice appearing on Jürgenson's tape, it must have been strong enough to affect the recording head of the machine. Thus 'PK at a distance' or 'telepsychokinesis' (TPK) was involved.

Although he has issued no formal pronouncement, Professor Bender inclines to the theory that TPK is behind most of the mystery voice phenomena. He feels that the voices may be PK emanating from the people present at a recording session; he points out that the voices that spoke to Raudive addressed him only in the languages with which he was familiar, and that American experimenters, for instance, tend to receive voices that speak with American accents.

He also quotes an incident that occurred during one of his own recording sessions. All the participants were wearing throat microphones attached to a separate tape recorder so that involuntary whispering could be monitored, and an engineer was taking oscillograph readings – visual voice recordings of everything heard on tape.

During the session, the name of a friend, Brigette Rasmus, came into Bender's mind. On playback, the tape contained the word 'Rasmus'; but the voice was not noticeably female. Bender was certain that it was not Brigette's, who was in any case alive and well in Germany, and both the throat-mike monitors and the oscillograph readings showed that he did not whisper the word. Yet

devoted two years between 1970 and 1972 to the scientific analysis of the voice phenomena. Subsequently he announced that, in half a dozen cases at least, he believed that Dr Raudive may have confused a Russian broadcast on Radio Luxembourg with his paranormal voices, but hastened to add that most of his 100,000 tapes were inexplicable in normal terms.

On 2 September 1974, Konstantin Raudive died at his home in Bad Krozingen. On 16 November, *Psychic News* carried a short report of a voice phenomenon experiment conducted at a conference on the paranormal in Germany some 10 days after his death. An American researcher set up a recorder and microphone, and subsequently the 130 delegates heard a voice, which many of them claimed to recognise as that of Raudive. Unfortunately the dead professor was no more specific than his painstakingly recorded voices had been, merely 'making apparent reference to "other techniques"'.

'We have no other details,' explained a spokesman for *Psychic News*. 'It is what we call a "question mark story".'

Other voices, other lives

It has long been known that under hypnosis some people regress to what appears to be a previous life. They not only assume another personality, but, as DAVID CHRISTIE-MURRAY shows, they can describe details from the past that are completely unknown to them outside of the trance state

HYPNOTIC REGRESSION into alleged previous lives is one of the most exciting and fascinating of psychic phenomena – and one of the most frustrating. During the past 20 years it has been brought to the attention of the general public every so often by programmes on radio and television, articles in the press and books written either by hypnotists themselves or by collaborators working with them.

Morey Bernstein's *The search for Bridey Murphy*, published in 1965, is still remembered if the small talk veers towards the occult; Arnall Bloxham's tapes, featured on radio and television programmes, and given a longer life by Jeffrey Iverson's *More lives than one?*, are widely known. Recently, Peter Moss has collaborated with Joe Keeton, prodigious in his expenditure of hypnotic man-hours, in the book *Encounters with the past*, which describes recordings of extracts from sessions with chosen subjects.

It is not generally realised that hypnotic regression into previous lives is not a recent discovery and has, in fact, been studied for nearly a century. The work of pioneers in this field, much of it lost because it was done long before the advent of the tape-recorder, is nevertheless valuable to students of reincarnation, whether they believe in it or not.

Travelling back in time

Part of the fascination of hypnotic regression lies in the very frustration that it engenders. Its revelations are both positive and negative,

some bolstering the faith of reincarnationists and puzzling sceptics, others bewildering believers and encouraging doubt. Regression is positive in that the dramatisations of former existences are vividly portrayed far beyond the acting abilities of subjects in their waking condition, so that observers repeatedly say: 'If this be acting, neither an Olivier or a Bernhardt could better it.'

Positive, too, is the consistency with which many subjects, regressed repeatedly to the same historical period, take up the previous life, so that the same personality, outlook and intonation of speech appear without effort or hesitation. The same incidents and facts are remembered even when trick questions are introduced to try to trap the speakers. This happens even when years separate the sessions.

Regression is positive in two further ways. The first is that obscure historical facts, apparently completely unknown beforehand to either hypnotist or subject and confirmed only after considerable research, are revealed in reply to general questions. An example of this is shown by one of Joe Keeton's subjects, Ann Dowling, an ordinary housewife who, during over 60 hours of regression, became Sarah Williams, an orphan living a life of utter squalor in a Liverpool slum in the first half of the 19th century.

When asked what was happening in Liverpool in 1850, Ann Dowling mentioned the visit of a foreign singer whose name had 'summat to do wi' a bird'. Research showed

Hypnotherapist Joe Keeton (top) has conducted more than 8000 regressions. One of his subjects, Ann Dowling (above), went back over 100 years and became Sarah Williams, who lived in Liverpool in the 1850s (top right). Among the facts recalled by Mrs Dowling was the visit of Swedish singer Jenny Lind (below)

that Jenny Lind, the 'Swedish Nightingale', on her way from Sweden to America, sang for two nights in Liverpool's Philharmonic Hall in August 1850.

The second positive aspect of hypnotic regression is found in the tiny details of past usage that slip naturally into the subject's conversation while reliving the past life. These details *might* have been picked up by the subject in his present lifetime and held in his subconscious memory, but they are unlikely to have been formally taught or known to people of ordinary education.

David Lowe, a member of the Society for Psychical Research, lectures about a woman whom he has regressed into a number of lives, some of them in different generations of the same family (an unusual feature), illustrating his talks with copious tape-recordings of her conversations in previous existences.

During a 17th-century regression, David Lowe asked the woman how a certain word containing a 'w' was spelt. Her spontaneous answer was 'double v' – the common pronunciation of the letter at that time. This

The belief in reincarnation

Tibetans believe that their spiritual leader, the Dalai Lama, is the reincarnation of a previous Dalai Lama whose soul enters the body of a child born at the precise moment of his death

The belief in reincarnation – that man's soul is reborn over and over again in another body or form – stretches far back into the past. The doctrine appears in primitive religions such as those of the Indian tribes of Assam, Nagas and Lushais, who believed that after death the soul took the form of an insect. The Bakongs of Borneo believed that their dead were reincarnated into the bearcats that frequented their raised coffins. The Kikuyu women of Kenya often worship at a place 'inhabited' by their ancestral souls in the belief that to become pregnant they must be entered by an ancestral soul.

According to Buddhist and Hindu thought man or the soul is reborn in accordance with merits acquired during his previous lifetime. But some sects of Hinduism hold that a man does not necessarily assume a human form in the next life. If he has been involved with vice or crime it is possible he may return as a cactus, toad, lizard, or even as poison ivy! The Buddhists believe that man is made up of elements: body, sensation, perception, impulse, emotion and consciousness, which fall apart at death. The individual, as such, ceases to exist and a new individual life begins according to the quality of the previous life, until at last achieving perfection and nirvana – eternal bliss.

Although reincarnation is not mentioned in Western texts until the late Greek and Latin writers, the idea dates back to at least the 6th century BC. It appears in the Orphic writings, which

appear to have played a great part in the thought of Pythagorus. He believed that the soul had 'fallen' into a bodily existence and would have to reincarnate itself through other forms to be set free. He himself claimed to have had previous existences including one as a soldier in a Trojan war.

Plato was greatly influenced by the Orphico-Pythagorean views and mentions reincarnation in his concluding part of the *Republic*. The soul, according to Plato, is immortal, the number of souls fixed, and reincarnation regularly occurs. Although discarded by Aristotle and other Stoic views, Plato's derivation was taken up by later schools of thought such as the Neoplatonists. Within the Christian church the belief was held by certain Gnostic sects during the first century AD and by the Manichaeans in the fourth and fifth centuries. But the idea was repudiated by eminent theologians at the time, and in AD 553, the Emperor Justinian condemned reincarnation, at the Second Council of Constantinople, as heresy.

Today the Westerner does have some difficulty in identifying with the Eastern idea of reincarnation. Most Western religious denominations share the view that the individual retains individuality after death, and finds the idea of returning as an animal or plant distinctly foreign. In 1917 the Roman Catholic Church denounced the idea as heresy.

Most adherents of reincarnation are now claiming the evidence from regressive hypnosis as proof for their case.

trivial detail was more telling to some listeners than all the researched dates and genealogies that substantiated the woman's story, remarkable as these were. When asked if she were engaged (to be married), the subject failed to understand the modern expression, but later talked happily of her recent betrothal.

Fact or fiction

The negative side of hypnotic regression is nevertheless considerable. There are many anachronisms, occasional historical howlers, instances of extraordinary ignorance and, with some subjects, inconsistencies (although much rarer than, and more balanced by, the consistencies).

One 19th-century character mentioned her 'boyfriend' in the modern sense of someone with a sexual love-interest in her. Another, regressed to the early 1830s and asked who ruled England, replied 'Queen Victoria', although four years of William IV's reign had still to run and Victoria's accession could not have been known for certain.

A common difficulty in substantiating historical facts is the scarcity of records of ordinary folk before the 19th century. Even when subjects mention landowners and comparatively important people, there is often no record of their existence in local archives. It is therefore sometimes extremely difficult to separate fact from fiction, especially as there may be a great deal of 'role-playing', the incubation in the subconscious mind of an imaginary personality around a nucleus of fact read in a history book or a novel.

Origins of modern hypnosis

Hypnosis is still so misunderstood and thought of as occult in the minds of many that it is as well to describe its place in modern thought.

Modern hypnosis began with Franz Mesmer, an Austrian physician who became a fashionable figure of Parisian society in the 18th century. He mistakenly believed that human beings emitted a force that could be transferred to objects such as iron rods. He 'magnetised' the rods by stroking them, then placed them in tubs filled with water in which his patients immersed their legs. Many and various were the ills allegedly cured by this method.

The extravagance of Mesmeric theory and its claims, together with the undertones of occultism that went with them, aroused intense opposition; and throughout the 19th century, serious investigators into hypnosis, and the few medical men bold enough to experiment with its use, met the kind of hostility once reserved for witches.

The Society for Psychical Research, which was founded in Britain in 1882, set up a committee to investigate hypnosis that continued to exist until a few years ago. Its findings, however, were not easily communicated to the general public and the phenomena it showed to be genuine were remarkable enough to maintain hypnotism's occult reputation, in spite of the Society's careful, objective and scholarly approach. But the therapeutic value of hypnosis was slowly established, especially in the treatment of psychological disorders.

After much investigation, it was discovered that subjects under hypnosis could be told either to *remember* what had happened on, say, their fifth birthday, or to *be* five years old again and to relive the day.

In the latter case, subjects would be led back to that day, write as they wrote at that age, relive the opening of their presents and each incident of the birthday party. They would have no knowledge of anything that happened after their fifth birthday until led forward by the hypnotist. It was as if all the layers of experience from five years old onwards had completely disappeared. The first man to attempt this age regression is said

The founder of modern hypnosis, Franz Anton Mesmer, believed that people emitted a force that could be transferred to iron rods. Parisians of all classes flocked to his salon in the 18th century where they sat round a large wooden tub called a *baquet*. This was filled with water, iron filings and bottles of 'magnetised' water. Projecting from the tub were iron rods, which patients held against their afflicted parts

to have been a Spaniard, Fernando Colavida, in 1887.

Further discoveries led to the investigation of pre-birth experiences in the womb and within a few years Dr Mortis Stark was studying the possibility of actually regressing subjects to a life before the present. At about the same time, in 1911, a Frenchman, Colonel Albert de Rochas, published an account of regressions that he had collected over several years.

A therapeutic role

The method employed in hypnotic regression is simple. After hypnotising the subject, the operator takes him back step by step to the beginning of his present life, then into the womb, and then instructs him to go back and back until he comes to some experience that he can describe. This is sometimes an 'existence' in the intermission between death ding a former life and birth beginning the present, sometimes experience of the former life itself, the period and circumstances of which the hypnotist can elicit by careful questioning.

The process is not merely used for interest's sake or to prove reincarnation – it can be therapeutic. Neuroses and other psychological disorders may be caused by traumas, the existence of which has been caused by shocks or other experiences in childhood or youth apparently too horrible for the conscious mind to face. To cure the neurosis, the trauma must be discovered and faced by the patient, and hypnosis is one technique able to dig it out.

By an extension of the process, neuroses and phobias may be caused by traumas experienced in alleged former lives that are revealed under hypnosis. Thus, one woman's terrible fear of water was caused by her having been bound with chains as a galley-slave in a previous existence, thrown into a river and eaten alive by crocodiles. A man terrified of descending in lifts had been a Chinese general who had accidentally fallen to his death from a great height. A young American girl about to dive from a high board was suddenly paralysed with fear after a moving bystander had been reflected in the water. Hypnosis revealed the hideous end of a former life in which she had been a girl in Florida who, just as she was jumping into the water, had seen the shadow of the alligator that was to devour her moving below the surface.

Whether or not these are memories of genuine previous experiences, they are convincing to many who have them. Much of the investigation into this particular aspect of hypnosis challenges the sceptics to find an explanation other than that of reincarnation. There *are* alternative explanations, which will be presented in future chapters.

Ten more lives to remember

Madame J, a soldier's wife and mother of one child, was delicate in health and as a girl had 'hated history'. She was regressed by Colonel de Rochas to 10 previous lives, some extremely detailed.

In the first she died at eight months. She then lived as a girl named Irisée in the country of the Imondo near Trieste. She next became a man, Esius, aged 40, who was planning to kill Emperor Probus in revenge for taking his daughter, Florina.

The fourth life was that of Carlomée, a Frankish warrior chieftain captured by Attila at Châlons-sur-Marne in AD 449. Abbess Martha followed, born in AD 923, who tyrannised young girls in a Vincennes convent as late as 1010. The Abbess was succeeded by Mariette Martin, aged 18 in 1300, daughter of a man who worked for the king – 'le beau Philippe'.

Madame J. then became Michel Berry, who was killed at the age of 22 in 1515 at the Battle of Marignano. This life was extremely detailed, Michel's career developing from his learning the art of fencing at 10, through his life as a page at the courts at Versailles and the Sorbonne and sundry love affairs to his presence aged 20 at the Battle of Guinegatte in Normandy.

Top: Colonel Albert de Rochas caused a sensation in 1911 with an account of hypnotic regression

Centre: the Emperor Probus, who was hated by Esius, the third personality in Madame J's previous lives

Above: the Battle of Marignano, in which Michel Berry died

After an eighth life as a wife and mother aged 30 in 1702, Madame J again became a man, Jules Robert. Jules was aged 38 in 1776 and a 'bad' worker in marble. Nevertheless one of his sculptures reached the Vatican.

Jules Robert reincarnated as Marguerite Duchesne, born in 1835, daughter of a grocer in the rue de la Caserne, Briançon. She went to school in the rue de la Gargouille. Research showed that the school existed, but there had never been a grocer Duchesne in the rue de la Caserne. Otherwise Madame J's description of places was accurate.

The case for Bridey Murphy

Have our lives been shaped not only by experiences and impressions gained since birth, but also by those from some other, previous existence?

IN 1956 AND 1957, Emile Franckel conducted a series of live experiments for a Los Angeles television programme called *Adventures in Hypnotism*. Franckel's aim was to bring to the public's attention the possibility that individuals under hypnosis can relive previous lives. His attitude was sceptical: he believed that recollections of previous lives arose from promptings from the hypnotist or deep subconscious memory. Some of the experiences he was able to draw from his subjects, however, seemed unaccountable by this explanation. Since the hypnotist did not know his subjects, he could scarcely have induced their responses except by a series of coincidences too remarkable to be statistically acceptable as mere chance.

Yet Franckel was right to have remained sceptical. For although some of the results were so remarkable as to seem almost miraculous, hypnosis is a mental state that almost anyone may experience given the right circumstances and which almost everyone can produce in at least some subjects – provided, of course, that he has mastered a few simple techniques – techniques that should never be used merely as a party game nor for exhibition purposes, nor by anyone who is unaware of its dangers. This does not

mean that hypnosis is fully understood by the medical profession. The following cases illustrate some of the areas where our knowledge is still inadequate in explaining regression into previous lives under hypnosis.

We assume that the human personality consists of potentialities derived from a combination of factors – parents' genes, plus, perhaps, racial memories and other elements. If reincarnation is ever to be established as fact, these 'other elements' will include memories of previous lives.

What appears to happen under hypnosis is that the layers of experience we have all acquired during our lives – experiences that have pushed our memory of previous existences deep into the subconscious – comes to the surface. When the hypnotist suggests, for example, to a 30-year-old subject: 'It is now 1970. You are now 20—you are waking up on your 20th birthday. Tell me where you are, what is happening', the subject's life and development of the past 10 years are as if they had never been.

Practising hypnotists know that no two subjects ever behave exactly alike, for all human beings are unique in some way, and with many subjects there seems to be a 'shadow' personality—a fantasy personality

Below: King Richard II (1367–1400) and courtiers at Conway Castle, Wales. In 1906 a clergyman's daughter claimed, while under hypnosis, to have lived a previous life in the court of Richard II and to have known his mother, the 'Fair Maid of Kent'

that is only revealed sometimes in dreams or under hypnosis. And, the suggestion is, it is this 'fantasy personality' that is revealed, not recollection of a previous life.

How are we to distinguish between what may be mere fantasy and a true account of a previous life? As early as 1906 the Society for Psychical Research reported the case of an unnamed clergyman's daughter who, under hypnosis, recounted her life during the reign of Richard II. In that life she was no great lady herself – despite the claim by cynics that *all* cases of regression imagine themselves to be famous people – but an acquaintance of Maud, Countess of Salisbury, her friend Blanche Poynings, née Mowbray, and Richard's mother, 'Fair Maid of Kent'.

In this case, almost every historical fact stated under hypnosis was found to be true, as were details of the dress and food described by the girl. Moreover, she had no recollection of ever having read about either the period or the people.

Some early psychical researchers into hypnotic phenomena awoke their subjects and placed their hands on a planchette board, usually screened from the subjects' view, and proceeded to interrogate them. The planchette – it is claimed – wrote down true answers to the questions from knowledge in the subjects' subconscious minds. Under these conditions the girl revealed that she had just read an historical romance in which every person and fact, except for some minor details, had appeared, though she had devised a new setting for them.

If all cases were as straightforward as this, there would be no need for further investigation, and believers in reincarnation would have to look elsewhere for evidence. How complicated the majority of cases are, however, is shown by the celebrated case of Bridey Murphy. This is no more remarkable than a hundred other cases of hypnotic regression, but was brought to the public's attention by a heated debate in a number of American newspapers and a film shown widely in English-speaking countries.

In a number of sessions from November 1952 to October 1953, Morey Bernstein, an amateur American hypnotist, regressed Mrs Virginia Tighe to a life in early 19th-century Ireland. Mrs Tighe, 29 years old at the time, a native of Madison, Wisconsin, and resident in Chicago from the age of three until her marriage, had never visited Ireland, nor had much to do with Irish people (she

Right: Morey Bernstein, the American hypnotist, and Mrs Virginia Tighe. The account given by Mrs Tighe of her 'previous life' as 'Bridey Murphy' led Morey Bernstein to become a firm believer in reincarnation

Below: a view of Cork as it was in the mid-18th century. It was here that Mrs Tighe claimed she had previously been born as 'Bridey Murphy' in 1798

Right: kissing the Blarney Stone in the manner described by Mrs Tighe. Today, all one does is to lie on the back, hold on to two bars attached to the wall, lower the head and kiss the underside of the Stone. The earlier method, used at the time of 'Bridey Murphy', would not have been known by Mrs Tighe without her having done a great deal of research

Below: to counter the claim that he had in some way rigged his experiments, Morey Bernstein hypnotised Mrs Tighe only in the presence of two witnesses

Bottom: uillean pipes of the type 'Bridey Murphy' claims were played at her funeral in Cork in 1864

strongly denied allegations to the contrary, and the evidence supports her denials). Under hypnosis she began to speak with an Irish accent, said she was Bridget (Bridey) Murphy, daughter of Duncan and Kathleen Murphy, Protestants living at the Meadows, Cork. Her brother Duncan, born in 1796, married Aimée, daughter of Mrs Strayne, who was mistress of a day school attended by Bridey when she was 15.

In about 1818 she married a Catholic, Brian MacCarthy, whose relatives she named, and they travelled by carriage to Belfast through places she named but whose existence has never been found on any map.

The couple worshipped at Father John Gorman's St Theresa's Church. They shopped at stores that Bridey named, using coins correctly described for the period. In addition, Bridey produced a number of Irish words when asked, using some as they were used then, though their meaning had changed since: 'slip', for example, referring to a child's pinafore, not petticoat – the more common modern word. Bridey Murphy had read some Irish mythology, knew some Irish songs and was a good dancer of Irish jigs. At the end of one sitting, Mrs Tighe, aroused from her trance, yet not fully conscious,

KISSING THE BLARNEY STONE.

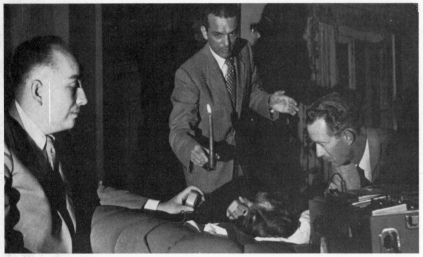

danced 'The Morning Jig', ending her performance with a stylised yawn. Her description of another dance was confirmed in detail by a lady whose parents had danced it. Another telling detail was that she described the correct procedure for kissing the Blarney Stone used in Bridey's day.

Bridey's story was investigated by the American magazine *Empire*. William Barker was commissioned by the magazine to spend three weeks in Ireland checking the facts 'Bridey' had given. His visit resulted in a 19,000-word report. Barker's account is typical of regression cases. Some facts were confirmed, others unconfirmed, others proved incorrect. Memories of insignificant detail proved true, while Bridey displayed total ignorance of other important events. Confirmation of facts proved impossible

in many instances. There was no possibility, for example, of confirming dates of birth, marriages and deaths, as no records were kept in Cork until 1864 and if the Murphy family kept records in a family Bible, a customary procedure, its whereabouts are not known. No information could be discovered concerning St Theresa's Church or Father Gorman in Belfast, but the two shops mentioned by Bridey, Carrigan and Farr, had both existed. Bridey had said that uillean pipes had been played at her funeral and these were found to have been customarily used at funerals because of their soft tone.

So the neutral enquirer is left puzzled. Where did Mrs Tighe learn about uillean pipes, kissing the Blarney Stone and the names of shops in Belfast whose existence was only confirmed after painstaking research? Why should she have created a vivid picture of life in Ireland at the beginning of the 19th century, if this was simply a creation of some part of her subconscious? From where did she – along with many other regressed subjects with no pretence at acting ability – draw the talent to dramatise so effectively a life in another age and another country?

Yet, if reincarnation is a fact, why should trivialities be remembered and great emotional experiences that one would have expected to have contributed to one's development in this life, be forgotten or go unmentioned? The questions are as bewildering as they are intriguing.